# TRANSFERENCE AND PROJECTION

## Core concepts in therapy

Series editor: Michael Jacobs

Over the last ten years a significant shift has taken place in the relations between representatives of different schools of therapy. Instead of the competitive and often hostile reactions we once expected from each other, therapists from different points of the spectrum of approaches are much more interested in where they overlap and where they differ. There is a new sense of openness to cross orientation learning.

The *Core Concepts in Therapy* series compares and contrasts the use of similar terms across a range of the therapeutic models, and seeks to identify where different terms appear to denote similar concepts. Each book is authored by two therapists, each one from a distinctly different orientation; and where possible each one from a different continent, so that an international dimension becomes a feature of this network of ideas.

Each of these short volumes examines a key concept in psychological therapy, setting out comparative positions in a spirit of free and critical enquiry, but without the need to prove one model superior to another. The books are fully referenced and point beyond themselves to the wider literature on each topic.

*Forthcoming and published titles*:
Geof Alred and Roger Ellis: *Words and Symbols*
Dinesh Bhugra and Dilys Davies: *Models of Psychopathology*
Paul Brinich and Christopher Shelley: *The Self and Personality Structure*
David Edwards and Michael Jacobs: *Conscious and Unconscious*
Dawn Freshwater and Chris Robertson: *Emotions and Needs*
Jan Grant and Jim Crawley: *Transference and Projection*
Richard J. Hazler and Nick Barwick: *The Therapeutic Environment*
Hilde Rapp and John Davy: *Resistance, Barriers and Defences*
John Rowan and Michael Jacobs: *The Therapist's Use of Self*
Lynn Seiser and Colin Wastell: *Interventions and Techniques*
Gabrielle Syme and Jenifer Elton Wilson: *Objectives and Outcomes*
Val Simanowitz and Peter Pearce: *Personality Development*
Nick Totton and Michael Jacobs: *Character and Personality Types*
Kenneth C. Wallis and James L. Poulton: *Internalization*

# TRANSFERENCE AND PROJECTION

Mirrors to the self

**Jan Grant**
**and**
**Jim Crawley**

**Open University Press**
Buckingham · Philadelphia

Open University Press
Celtic Court
22 Ballmoor
Buckingham
MK18 1XW

email: enquiries@openup.co.uk
world wide web: www.openup.co.uk

and
325 Chestnut Street
Philadelphia, PA 19106, USA

First Published 2002

A catalogue record of this book is available from the British Library

ISBN   0 335 20315 9 (hb)   0 335 20314 0 (pb)

*Library of Congress Cataloging-in-Publication Data*
    Grant, Jan, 1951–
      Transference and projection : mirrors to the self / Jan Grant and Jim
      Crawley.
        p. cm. – (Core concepts in therapy)
      Includes bibliographical references and index.
      ISBN 0-335-20315-9 – ISBN 0-335-20314-0 (pbk.)
      1. Transference (Psychology)   2. Projection (Psychology)
    I. Crawley, Jim.   II. Title.   III. Series.

    RC489.T73 G73 2002
    616.89′14–dc21                                            2001059323

Typeset by Graphicraft Limited, Hong Kong
Printed in Great Britain by The Cromwell Press, Trowbridge

**To**
**Guy, Serena and Kirsty**
**Shirley, Karen, Rebecca and Cameron**

# Contents

*Series editor's preface*                                           xi
*Preface*                                                          xv
*Acknowledgements*                                                xix

**1  Mirrors to the self: an introduction to transference**        1
   Introducing transference                                        1
   A working definition of transference                            4
   Transference and the unconscious                                5
   Why is transference important?                                  6
   Three major ways of understanding transference                  8
   Communicating the transference                                  9
   Transference and brief psychotherapy                           11
   Using transference and projection to understand the
      internal self                                               12
   Promotion of the transference                                  12
   Working with transference and projection                       13
   Resistance to transference                                     13
   Interpretations and transference                               14
   Conclusion                                                     16

**2  Projection and projective identification**                   18
   Introduction                                                   18
   Projection                                                     20
   Projection in daily life                                       22
   Projection in cyberspace                                       23
   Projection in therapy groups                                   24
   Projective identification                                      26

Why is projective identification important? 30
Some principles in working with projective
    identification 31
Conclusion 33

**3 Early development of the understanding of
transference** 34
Introduction 34
Freud's discovery of transference 35
Transference in the work of Melanie Klein 41

**4 Developments in understanding transference:
psychodynamic psychotherapies** 46
Introduction 46
Object relations 46
    Working with transference in object relations
        therapy 48
Self psychology 51
    Working with transference in self psychology 53
Intersubjective approaches 55
    Working with transference from an intersubjective
        perspective 55
Brief psychodynamic psychotherapy 57
    Working with transference in brief psychodynamic
        therapy 58
Conclusion 60

**5 Schemas and scripts: cognitive-behavioural therapy
and transference** 62
Introduction 62
Cognitive-behavioural therapy and the therapeutic
    relationship 63
Schema and script theory 63
Transference phenomena as *in vivo* interventions 67
Cognitive therapy approaches to understanding
    transference 68
Working with 'transference' in cognitive-behavioural
    therapy 69
Working with 'projection' in cognitive-behavioural
    therapy 72
Conclusion 73

**6 The real relationship: transference and humanistic-existential/experiential therapies** 74
Introduction 74
Person-centred/humanistic approaches 75
Existential and experiential approaches 77
Gestalt therapy 82
Gestalt therapy, projection and projective
identification 85
Psychodrama 86
Conclusion 90

**7 The transference prism: couples and family therapy** 92
Introduction 92
Understanding couple and family relationships 96
The process of conjoint therapy 103
A resource for facilitating change in relationships 107
Conclusion 112

**8 Recognizing and responding to transference** 113
Introduction 113
The essential features of transference 114
Transference as an unconscious organizing activity 114
The complex origins of transference 115
Transference involves persistent perceptions of the
other 116
Recognizing transference 117
Positive and negative transferences 117
Erotic transference 119
Selfobject transferences: mirroring, idealizing and
twinship transferences 121
The two triangles of transference 123
Transference and change 128
Responding to transference and projection 131
Conclusion 134

*References* 136
*Index* 149

# Series editor's preface

A major aspect of intellectual and cultural life in the twentieth century has been the study of psychology – present of course for many centuries in practical form and expression in the wisdom and insight to be found in spirituality, in literature and in the dramatic arts, as well as in arts of healing and guidance, both in the East and West. In parallel with the deepening interest in the inner processes of character and relationships in the novel and theatre in the nineteenth century, psychiatry reformulated its understanding of the human mind, and encouraged, in those brave enough to challenge the myths of mental illness, new methods of exploration of psychological processes.

The second half of the twentieth century in particular witnessed an explosion of interest both in theories about personality, psychological development, cognition and behaviour, as well as in the practice of therapy, or perhaps more accurately, the therapies. It also saw, as is not uncommon in any intellectual discipline, battles between theories and therapists of different persuasions, particularly between psychoanalysis and behavioural psychology, and each in turn with humanistic and transpersonal therapies, as well as within the major schools themselves. Such arguments are not surprising, and indeed objectively can be seen as healthy – potentially promoting greater precision in research, alternative approaches to apparently intractable problems, and deeper understanding of the wellsprings of human thought, emotion and behaviour. It is nonetheless disturbing that for many decades there was such a degree of sniping and entrenchment of positions from therapists who should have been able to look more closely at their own responses and rivalries. It is as if diplomats had ignored their skills and knowledge and resorted in their dealings with each other to gun slinging.

The psychotherapeutic enterprise has also been an international one. There were a large number of centres of innovation, even at the beginning – Paris, Moscow, Vienna, Berlin, Zurich, London, Boston USA – and soon Edinburgh, Rome, New York, Chicago and California saw the development of different theories and therapeutic practice. Geographical location has added to the richness of the discipline, particularly identifying cultural and social differences, and widening the psychological debate to include, at least in some instances, sociological and political dimensions.

The question has to be asked – given the separate developments due to location, research interests, personal differences, and splits between and within traditions – whether what has sometimes been called 'psycho-babble' is indeed a welter of different languages describing the same phenomena through the particular jargon and theorizing of the various psychotherapeutic schools. Or are there genuine differences, which may lead sometimes to the conclusion that one school has got it right, while another has therefore got it wrong; or that there are 'horses for courses'; or, according to the Dodo principle, that 'all shall have prizes'?

The latter part of the twentieth century saw some rapprochement between the different approaches to the theory and practice of psychotherapy (and counselling), often due to the external pressures towards organizing the profession responsibly and to the high standards demanded of it by health care, by the public and by the state. It is out of this budding rapprochement that there came the motivation for this series, in which a number of key concepts that lie at the heart of the psychotherapies can be compared and contrasted across the board. Some of the terms used in different traditions may prove to represent identical concepts; others may look similar, but in fact highlight quite different emphases, which may or may not prove useful to those who practise from a different perspective; other terms, apparently identical, may prove to mean something completely different in two or more schools of psychotherapy.

In order to carry out this project it seemed essential that as many of the psychotherapeutic traditions as possible should be represented in the authorship of the series; and to promote both this, and the spirit of dialogue between traditions, it seemed also desirable that there should two authors for each book each one representing, where practicable, different orientations. It was important that the series should be truly international in its approach and therefore in its authorship; and that miracle of late twentieth-century technology, the Internet, proved to be a productive means of finding authors, as well as a remarkably efficient method of communicating, in the cases of some pairs of authors, halfway across the world.

This series therefore represents, in a new millennium, an extremely exciting development, one which as series editor I have found more and more enthralling as I have eavesdropped on the drafts shuttling back and forth between authors. Here, for the first time, the reader will find all the major concepts of all the principal schools of psychotherapy and counselling (and not a few minor ones) drawn together so that they may be compared, contrasted, and (it is my hope) above all used – used for the ongoing debate between orientations; but more importantly still, used for the benefit of clients and patients who are not at all interested in partisan positions, but in what works, or in what throws light upon their search for healing and understanding.

*Michael Jacobs*

# Preface

The subtitle to this book, 'mirrors to the self', captures the essence of why transference and projection are such important phenomena in psychotherapy. It is through experiencing and understanding the unconscious processes of transference and projection that the inner world of the client can be glimpsed and the structure of the self partially revealed. This process is more akin to a hall of mirrors, where reflections of reflections present a multitude of pictures – some of which are elongated, widened or distorted in other ways that resemble, but are not perfect copies of, the original image. Transference and projection are processes that occur in therapy that mean that the past comes alive in the here-and-now moment of the relationship between therapist and client. The unconscious templates or schemas that individuals use to organize their wishes, fantasies, beliefs and constructs about their relationships can be best understood and worked with when they are 'alive' in the room and directed towards the therapist.

This book brings together different views of transference and projection, first from the psychodynamic therapies where the constructs originated and then from the perspective of other major models of psychotherapy. Although not all models of therapy use the terms 'transference' and 'projection', they all have something important to say about working with transference-like phenomena in the therapeutic enterprise.

The book begins by introducing transference and projection through clinical material and the more generic understandings of the phenomena. It explains what transference is, why it is significant in the therapeutic enterprise and what forms it takes. Chapter 2 focuses on two particular forms of transferential phenomena – projection and projective identification – and how they make an appearance in therapy, in family life and in the wider social system. Chapter 3 considers the origins of the concepts of transference, projection and projective identification in the beginnings of the psychoanalytic world of Freud and then Klein. Chapter 4 focuses on subsequent developments in theory and practice within the psychodynamic frameworks of object-relations, self psychology and intersubjective approaches and how such approaches have added rich layers of understanding of the phenomenon. The remaining chapters describe how transference and projection are conceptualized and worked with in the three other major models of therapy. Chapter 5 considers developments within the cognitive-behavioural therapies that have recently begun to address more seriously the therapeutic relationship, including transference and projection phenomena. This has partially come about as the model is extended to more complex populations such as those with personality disorders. Chapter 6 discusses the humanistic-existential therapies, their understanding and methods of working with transference, and how this fits with their focus on the 'real relationship' between client and therapist. Chapter 7 brings to life the developments in couples/family therapy that have helped us to understand firmly entrenched patterns of projection in long-term relationships and how these may be worked with to enhance therapeutic gains. The final chapter summarizes the essential features of transference and projection and then considers how psychotherapists and counsellors can recognize and respond to transference and projection in ways that enhance the therapeutic relationship.

The purpose of the book is to provide a clear understanding of these clinical phenomena for those studying to become counsellors or psychotherapists, as well as for those experienced practitioners who may be less familiar with such phenomena. We have used many clinical examples from our own practices as psychotherapists to illuminate the kinds of complex processes we are trying to clarify theoretically. We hope that the book also provides a review for those clinicians who already work extensively with transference but who may not be aware of how other models of therapy are currently dealing with transference and projection. In this respect, the book also aims to contribute to the growing literature on psychotherapy integration. Although we value the differences between individual models of therapy, we also believe that the field is now mature enough to begin to look seriously at the overlaps between models, both technically and theoretically. Certainly, in training psychotherapists and counsellors we want to ensure that new clinicians are able to draw appropriately on more than one approach to therapy. On the other hand, we are not advocating a sloppy eclecticism that doesn't take account of serious philosophical or theoretical differences between models. Rather, we hope that the book assists clinicians to position themselves in their favoured model, yet be able to use some of the wisdom that is situated in the rich understandings of the therapeutic relationship from other models.

# Acknowledgements

We would like to express our gratitude to our clients. They have been our teachers in understanding what works in psychotherapy and how the therapeutic relationship impacts on the work of therapy. For those clients whose stories – with details disguised to protect confidentiality – appear as extended clinical vignettes in this book, we are especially appreciative for both their commitment to the therapeutic process and their willingness to allow their stories to be told. It is through their stories that the theory underpinning therapy comes to life and assists other clinicians to understand the clinical phenomena described. Although the focus of therapy is on change in the client, it is also true that, in an extended and powerful therapy, the therapist also changes. The therapeutic relationship has a significant impact, both on the client and the therapist.

We would also like to express our appreciation to our most 'significant others' – our spouses, Guy Grant and Shirley Crawley – who have both in their individual ways unerringly supported us in our work as therapists, academics and in the writing of this book. They have provided the 'secure base' from which we can explore the world of psychotherapy. We would also like to thank our children – now mostly adult – for teaching us first hand about human development and the intensity of the lifetime bonds of love. Jan Grant would also like to thank Dave and Sandy Gauntlett, my mother and father for teaching me that life is to be fully lived, family is to be enjoyed and laughter is central.

Others have given us good advice and feedback on various chapters in the book. We would like to thank Lynette Clayton, Paul McEvoy, Lee Goddard-Williams, Andrew Ralph and Neville Sparrow who read and responded to the material from their perspective as psycho-therapists. We thank them for their clinical wisdom and astute comments that helped us to sharpen our thinking and writing. In addition, Michael Jacobs, the series editor, has been extremely helpful in his sensitive and wise editing of the material; we thank him for this and also for his patience in awaiting the completion of the final manuscript.

More broadly, psychotherapists, supervisors, colleagues and, of course, friends have been highly influential in our development as psychotherapists. We would like to acknowledge some of these individuals, for without them we may not have developed ourselves or the clinical wisdom that has made psychotherapy for us such an engrossing activity. For their support, encouragement and shared wisdom, we thank Lynette Clayton, Lekkie Hopkins, Robert van Koesveld, Paul McEvoy, Gally McKenzie, Paige Porter, Sherry Saggers, Chris Theunissen, Margaret Topham and Wendy-Lynn Wolman.

We would like to acknowledge the support of Curtin University of Technology and Edith Cowan University in providing each of us with a semester of study leave; this allowed us to write most of the book away from the demands and challenges of teaching and administration at the university. Our teaching of psychotherapy has been central to who we are as professionals. Finally, we thank our students and supervisees over the years for their constructive feedback, which has sharpened our focus and pushed us to become clearer as we try to articulate the world of therapy in ways that make sense to them.

*Jan Grant*
*Jim Crawley*

# Mirrors to the self: an introduction to transference

## Introducing transference

Psychotherapy is a fascinating and intimate enterprise that revolves around a special kind of relationship developed between the therapist and the client. This therapeutic relationship has many facets, all important to the effectiveness of therapy. One particularly significant aspect of this relationship is when the client unconsciously reacts to the therapist from patterns established early in life. Transference is the label given to such experiences in the therapeutic endeavour. Take the following example:

> Daniel arrived cold, wet and late for his weekly psychotherapy session, saying his car had broken down. The therapist was sympathetic about his difficulties, especially since it was raining hard, and offered him a hot cup of tea before the start of the session. At the end of the session, Daniel asked her to drive him home, since it was the last session of the day and it was dark and wet outside. She gently refused, saying it would not be appropriate to drive him home, but that he could use her phone to call his partner. In subsequent sessions, Daniel (who had been seeing his therapist weekly for 3 years) expressed considerable hurt and anger that she had not 'cared enough' about him to do what he considered this very simple favour. Although he understood the therapeutic process and the importance of boundaries, he felt that she had rigidly considered her own needs over his. It took several sessions to come to the understanding that, for Daniel, this experience

was like his relationship with his mother, where as a child he had been left alone in the house for long periods of time to cope by himself. When she was present, her needs were large and took priority over his. He felt she had not 'cared enough' about his needs for emotional and physical support at a time when he was too young to care for his own.

What is happening here and why is it important to the progress of therapy? In essence, Daniel has experienced a gentle but firm 'no' to his request for practical physical assistance as abandonment by his therapist and a signal that she, like others in his life, does not 'care enough' about his needs. This leads to an exacerbation of his depressive symptoms as he re-experiences the old feelings of being alone and too little to look after himself. As in many instances of transference, there is a precipitating event in the therapy that is then 'read', by the client, through the template of previous relationship experiences. Such templates are organized, internalized schemas that operate at an unconscious level – that is, the client is not aware of the process, even if their attention is drawn to it. Events like the one described above will impede the progress of therapy if they are not processed in ways that can be understood by the client. If Daniel continues to experience his therapist as cold and non-caring about his needs, there will be a rupture in the 'working alliance' and the therapy is likely to be stalled.

Difficulties in adult relatedness often stem from relationships with early care-givers that were disappointing, frustrating or, perhaps, frightening and abusive. Attachment theory (Bowlby 1969, 1988) shows us how the attachment relationship to a primary care-giver meets the child's basic needs for nurturance, modulates the negative effects of anxiety and fosters healthy development. These early experiences lead to schemas or mental representations of relationship and of what is needed to maintain a connection with other people. These become organized, encoded experiential and cognitive data. Continuity is maintained by enacting these patterns of social interaction in ways that lead to self-confirmation (Grant and Porter 1994; Levenson 1995; Grant 2000). Indeed, transference refers both to the tendency to experience the relationship with the therapist in similar ways to the relationship with early care-givers and to the tendency to structure re-enactments of early disturbing relationships. This was named the 'repetition compulsion' by Freud (1912).

In the psychodynamic models of therapy, experiencing, understanding and interpreting the transference is considered a core element in engendering client change. According to Merton Gill (1982), therapeutic movement results when clients re-experience and express archaic thoughts, feelings and impulses in the presence of the therapist to whom they are now directed, and are able to have that expression met with interest, objectivity and acceptance. However, intellectual understanding about those patterns is not enough. Transference means that these early patterns re-emerge and are re-experienced in relation to the therapist; this helps the client to grasp at an experiential level just how pervasive they are (Kahn 1997). The experience of a different response to the original archaic feelings than that provided by the early care-giver is also central to the change process (Grant and Crawley 2001).

Transference does not just occur in the therapy relationship. Transference is ubiquitous (Andersen and Berk 1998; Book 1998) – it occurs in marital relationships, with friends, lovers, bosses, doctors and others. We expect others to respond to us as we have been treated before, by our mother, father or siblings and other significant figures. Consequently, we behave according to those expectations (Grant 2000). For example:

> Mark gets highly anxious when his wife Mary spends time with a particular group of friends. Mary's friends are very extroverted and Mark worries that she, like his mother, will abandon him to pursue more interesting activities and people. He exhibits this anxiety through attempts to control her contact with them, until, with the help of therapy, he begins to see the connections between his anxiety and his relationship with his mother. Through couple's therapy, Mark is able to express his fears and Mary is able to reassure him that he is the person she wants to be with. Mark's transference can be seen in how he interprets Mary's behaviour – in line with his previous experiences with his mother. Without realizing it, he constructs his experience with Mary as being similar to his experience with his mother and this brings into play similar feelings of anxiety about abandonment.

Although transference has traditionally been explored in relation to psychopathology, it is not inherently pathological. Rather, it is part of the human process of making meaning that helps humans to predict, understand and make sense of interpersonal events (Andersen and Berk 1998). It is more often the content of the transference that is maladaptive in shaping people's interpersonal world than the process of transference itself. For example, if as a child you learned to be compliant to 'keep the peace' in a volatile family, you may find yourself being compliant with friends or your boss. The process of learning to be compliant served a particular purpose in a dysfunctional family environment – but the content of such a schema is maladaptive as a mature, independent adult, where such conditions do not exist.

## A working definition of transference

Although transference is ubiquitous, it has a special meaning in the context of the therapeutic relationship. Gelso and Hayes (1998: 11) define transference as 'the client's experience of the therapist that is shaped by his or her own psychological structures and past, and involves displacement onto the therapist, of feelings, attitudes, and behaviors belonging rightfully in earlier significant relationships'. Transference includes the feelings towards the therapist, but also how the client expects to behave and feel and what the client expects from the therapist. For example, the client may expect the therapist to like or love them, to disapprove of them, to understand them, to abuse, manipulate or abandon them. Clients may distort the therapist's behaviour to conform to these expectations. Alternatively, clients may behave towards the therapist in ways that actually produce such reactions. In general terms, transference is often linked to unresolved issues with significant figures in one's past; it can be helpful, neutral or destructive to therapy, depending upon the extent to which it is recognized and how it is responded to by the therapist (Gelso and Hayes 1998).

Transference, however, is not simply a distortion or a repetition of the past. It is the client's interpretation of a therapeutic interaction. In the example at the start of this chapter, there was a precipitating event where Daniel asked the therapist to drive him home and she refused. Daniel interpreted the interaction in terms of both his past and current experience. In his current experience, he expected the therapist, as a person who had shown concern with his welfare, to be compassionate and to put aside her commitment to therapeutic boundaries this one time. When she gently refused, he re-experienced the same feelings of hurt, anger and aloneness that he had experienced repeatedly as a child. This is an example of what Dorpat and Miller (1992) refer to as 'organizing schemata', which provide the transference with an experiential component. Daniel's interpretation that this meant that, like his mother, the therapist was not willing to put his needs before hers and that she too was therefore 'uncaring' when he needed her, is his best interpretation of the event given his past history. Dorpat and Miller (1992) refer to this as a 'conceptual schema', because it gives an interpretive meaning to the event.

These concepts help to explain transference as an organizing activity that all humans engage in to help make sense of the multitude of interactions and experiences over a lifetime. Indeed, Freud, who initially identified transference in his early work as a doctor and then clarified it in his work with 'Dora', grew to think of it as a 'template'. He saw the transference template as a core relationship pattern that provided a prototype or schema for interactions in subsequent relationships (Luborsky and Crits-Christoph 1998). Andersen and Berk (1998) argue that such patterns learned early in life influence current behaviour because they are stored in memory and are then activated and applied to other relationships. For example, the gendered expectations about marital care that occur within a marital relationship often operate at an unconscious level, which make them difficult to shift (Grant and Porter 1994; Grant 2000).

In this respect, transference begins to sound very similar to 'psychological schemas' described in social psychology or cognitive-behavioural psychology. A psychological schema is 'an enduring symbolic framework that organizes constellations of thought, feeling, memory, and expectation about self and others' (Knapp 1991: 94).

## Transference and the unconscious

Transference is largely an unconscious process. That is, individuals are unaware that they are projecting past experiences and understandings onto the current situation. There is now considerable research evidence to show that individuals use automatic and unconscious processes when transference is operating (Andersen 1995). Part of the process of psychodynamic psychotherapy is helping the client to become aware of and understand their transferential material, thereby 'making the unconscious, conscious'. This is particularly important when the experiential and conceptual schemas used by the client are maladaptive, because such reactions will inevitably be occurring in other interpersonal interactions in the client's life.

Stolorow *et al.* (1994) argue that, as young children, we must find a way of organizing the multitude of experiences we have with others. We are strongly influenced by those closest to us – our parents, teachers, care-givers and siblings. We form unconscious principles to organize all the stimuli. For Daniel, in the example above, an organizing principle was that others never responded appropriately to his needs. Because these organizing principles operate outside of awareness, it feels as if we are simply responding to the current situation in a realistic manner. Therapy helps us to bring them into awareness and have more choices about how we respond to others.

Daniel Stern (1998), in his evocative book about mother–infant psychotherapy, describes in some detail how these 'schemas' or 'working models' develop in the earliest interactions between mother and baby. For example, he describes how infants of depressed mothers attempt to reanimate the mother:

> He vocalizes, smiles, gestures, and is often very creative with humor and invention. When none of this works, he turns his head away for a moment and then turns back to try again . . . The important point about this envelope of infant behaviors is that it sometimes works and the mother is reanimated, even though depressed.

> (Stern 1998: 102)

Over time, some infants develop a pattern of reanimation that can lead to developing a personality around being a 'charmer'. Stern argues that these moments develop a 'schema-of-being', which, if continually repeated, develop into working models or role relationship models. This then forms the basis for transference once these internal models are reactivated in the therapeutic relationship.

### Why is transference important?

Transference is one of the cornerstones of psychodynamically oriented therapies. Transference assists the therapist to understand the past in terms of the origins of conflicts and difficulties, and to observe the ways that the past is alive in the present. The past presents itself in the here-and-now of the therapeutic relationship, which is what Jacobs (1998) calls the 'living laboratory' of therapy. Therapists are presented with opportunities to 're-experience with their clients certain aspects of their presenting past; in which the effects of the past can be reviewed; and through which the effects can be to some extent adapted to the new circumstances of the present and the future' (Jacobs 1998: 285). Through transference, clients experience the strong positive and negative feelings belonging to the schema that they have developed within their early relationships. Working with this material in therapy becomes the crucible that produces insight, intrapsychic change and change in interpersonal patterns. Thus, transference is highly valued for its capacity to crystallize current interpersonal patterns and past conflicts that continue to organize current experience (Grant 1997; Grant and Crawley 2001).

In contemporary psychoanalytic thinking, there has been a profound shift in emphasis from interpreting the unconscious elements of the past to examining how the past is alive in the present. There is more focus on capturing and interpreting the here-and-now relationship between client and therapist (Gill 1982, 1994; Holmes 1998). Transference is seen as the mobilization, in the here-and-now, of psychological dynamics that originated in the there-and-then. This assists clients to become aware of the range of their responses and to open up greater possibilities for more adaptive responses. This is not dissimilar to cognitive therapy, where there is a focus on becoming aware of and changing automatic processes that lead to maladaptive thought patterns.

Transference is important whatever the form of therapy and even if the construct is not part of the therapeutic model. Transference-like phenomena create misunderstandings and impasses in therapy, frequently leading to premature termination. Studies involving retrospective recall of unresolved misunderstandings in therapy show that they typically involve transference-like phenomena, whatever the form of therapy (Rhodes *et al.* 1994). It is suggested that, whatever model is used, the therapist still must pay attention to both covert and overt responses to themselves.

This is particularly important when such responses threaten to disrupt the 'working alliance'. The 'working alliance' (Greenson 1967) or 'therapeutic alliance' (Zetzel 1958) describes the bond that develops between the client and therapist. This alliance is imperative to the progress of any therapeutic endeavour. The development of such a bond is assisted through therapist activity such as empathy, clarification, non-judgementalness and understanding. Indeed, in some schools of therapy, such as self psychology or person-centred counselling, the relationship itself is seen as an important curative element. The therapeutic alliance means there is a joint commitment to working together to understand and address the difficulties of the client. Transference phenomena can disrupt this bond and, unless addressed, can lead to impasses, resistance, sabotage, absences and eventually termination.

Transference is essentially a psychoanalytic concept and thus some of the richest understandings about it have come from psychoanalytic writers. However, most models of therapy have described transference phenomena, but have engaged somewhat different terminology to describe, understand and prescribe ways of dealing with such phenomena. Subsequent chapters will trace how both psychoanalytic theory and other models describe and deal with such phenomena therapeutically.

## Three major ways of understanding transference

The notion of transference was first discussed by Freud, when he discovered that patients in psychoanalysis would begin to treat him as if he were a significant figure from their childhood. Transference grew to become a central construct in psychoanalysis and the 'working through' of the transference is currently considered the cornerstone of all psychoanalytically oriented psychotherapies. Since the discovery of transferential phenomena in the late 1800s, the concept has undergone many revisions, and now there are several different schools of thought on what transference is and how it might best be worked with and understood. These different ways of understanding transference fall into three broad categories.

The first is the classical view held by Freudian psychoanalysts. This view posits that transference is a re-experiencing of early intrapsychic conflicts centred on oedipal issues. Oedipal issues refer to the psychosexual conflicts experienced as a child deals with their wishes, fantasies and fears in relation to their parents. Here the therapist is reacted to as if they are one of the participants in the client's early oedipal environment. Transference, here, is the wish to gratify early childhood desires that were directed towards the parents, but have remained unconscious and have often created internal conflicts. These feelings can be highly negative or erotically charged positive feelings towards the therapist. The therapist becomes the focus of unfulfilled or conflictual wishes (Scharfman 1992).

The second is the view that has emerged from the relational schools of psychoanalysis, including object-relations, ego-analytic and interpersonal schools. This view suggests that transference is a repetition of early significant relationships. Feelings, fantasies and behaviours that belong with early relationships are reactivated in therapy and experienced in relation to the therapist. This perspective places greater emphasis on the adaptability of the original response given the care-taking environment. The original response is seen as having been appropriate in terms of self-protection, protection of the child's self-esteem, or making the environment more tolerable. Transference is seen as a reactivation of critical relationship patterns in early life and is, therefore, seen as crucial to the therapeutic process (Grant 1997; Grant and Crawley 2001).

The third and most recent view moves beyond the definition of transference as distortion. In the intersubjective schools of thought, transference is seen as a process that is contributed to by both therapist and client. The intersubjective reality is 'co-constructed' through conscious and unconscious contributions of both parties. The therapist's job is to assist the client in understanding the reality they have jointly constructed. The client slowly incorporates the therapeutic relationship and this helps them to restructure their internal subjective world. Much of the focus here is on how the client's experience of the relationship is directed by their own psychological organization. This view, more than the others, emphasizes transference as an organizing activity used by all humans.

## Communicating the transference

There are several ways that clients communicate their transferential experiences to the therapist (Dorpat and Miller 1992; Luborsky and Crits-Christoph 1998). These can be categorized into three major modes of representation. The first mode is direct, whereby the client actually tells the therapist how he is experiencing her. For example:

At the beginning of the session, Jane, a young adult, says that she left the previous session quite disturbed. At the end of the previous session, as she was leaving, Jane said that her therapist had smiled at her and laughed as she said goodbye. Jane said she thought that this meant that her therapist was laughing at her because she was strange, 'not normal', and somewhat crazy. Jane was depressed and disturbed by this all week and felt that her therapist had become very critical of her. As the therapist reflected on what Jane was saying, she could remember smiling at Jane at the end of the previous session, feeling positive about the work together, and possibly chuckling fondly with her as she said goodbye. She had no memory of feeling judgemental towards her. Much of the current session was spent exploring the meaning of Jane's experience. Jane had a history of being severely bullied and isolated in her early school years, where other children called her names and said she was strange. In addition, Jane's father was highly critical of her and found it difficult to respond positively to any progress Jane made. After exploring these connections, near the end of the session the therapist let Jane know what she remembered of the interaction. These instances of 'reality-testing' were important to Jane in helping her to discriminate between people's reactions to her, where she was often hypersensitive.

In this example, Jane transfers her childhood experiences of being laughed at, teased and bullied by other children onto her therapist's behaviour. She also, in these moments, experiences her therapist, like her father, as being critical and judgemental of her progress. She reads her therapist's behaviour through the lens of childhood trauma. Because the therapeutic alliance is strong, Jane is able to tell her therapist about this and to tolerate exploration of the feelings and where they are coming from.

A second mode of communication of transference is symbolic, through stories or descriptions of events in the client's life. Sometimes these stories are symbolic of the transference relationship with the therapist. For example:

Cathy is nearing termination of three years of therapy that she has found quite helpful. She is having a hard time directly thanking her therapist for their work together, saying goodbye and articulating the changes. Instead, she talks extensively about how her clinical supervisor at work will be on leave for a month, but how she feels capable of coping without him now. She says how helpful this supervisor has been, but she realizes that she is 'big enough' now as a professional to cope on her own without that support, that she now has an 'internal supervisor'. Even though there are some difficulties at work, she feels less anxious about managing them herself. Her therapist offers an interpretation: 'Perhaps you are also saying that you are "big enough" now to manage your personal problems on your own, without me; that you have developed enough capacity and strength through this process to cope, without support, but it is hard to say that so directly to me'. Cathy's eyes fill with tears and she agrees with this.

Here, there is an 'allusion to the transference' (Gill 1982) through the story about the supervisor. There is clearly a strong symbolic connection between ending therapy and feeling capable enough to cope by oneself and the experience of the supervisor going on leave. The indirectness, in this case, is also an unconscious mechanism that works to avoid the sadness and intimacy of saying goodbye to the therapist.

The third mode of transference communication is through images such as dreams and fantasies. Here the client may report a dream or fantasy with the therapist actually in it, or may talk about a dream where there is clearly a symbolic representation of the therapeutic relationship.

A fourth mode is that of 'enactment', where a client enacts a particular early role relationship with the therapist. The first clinical example in this chapter with the client Daniel is an illustration of an enactment. Daniel actually enacted the role relationship he had with his mother, by asking the therapist to take care of his physical needs in ways that would be rejected by the therapist. Daniel nudges the therapist into a countertransference enactment where they reciprocally live out his internalized roles (Hirsch 1998). He then re-experiences towards the therapist both his original wish to be taken care of by his mother and his feelings of depression when she does not attend to him in developmentally appropriate ways.

## Transference and brief psychotherapy

The phenomenon of transference was originally thought to emerge primarily under the conditions of psychoanalysis. Here, frequency of contact with the therapist (three to five times a week), length of treatment (usually over a number of years) and therapist neutrality and minimal intervention were assumed to create the conditions for the emergence of transference as well as the 'working through' of the transference.

More recently, however, brief models of psychodynamic psychotherapy have emerged that also hold transference as central to their diagnostic and curative processes (Gustafson 1997; Book 1998). These therapies are time-limited, generally lasting somewhere between twelve and forty sessions. Transference is promoted early in the therapy and dealt with in the context of the core issues being pursued. It is promoted through bringing the client's attention to any direct, symbolic or veiled allusion to the therapist and connections are made early between such processes and the core issue of the client. It is also promoted through examining the client's responses towards the therapist in the context of the core issue. If the definition of transference as a ubiquitous organizing activity is used, it makes sense that the client's responses and reactions to the therapist will in part be derived from the templates about relationship that they use. Thus, although a longer-term therapy is likely to produce a greater intensity and complexity in the transference, brevity is no impediment to the emergence of transferential phenomena.

Indeed, short-term psychotherapy has been an important impetus in the development of a focus on the here-and-now transference. This focus helps a client to understand and work through interpersonal patterns that generate conflict or difficulty. The crucial change agent in such therapies is an intensive emphasis on working through the transference (Bauer and Mills 1994).

## Using transference and projection to understand the internal self

The processes of transference and projection are crucial to therapy because they provide a mirror to the internal self. Our most profound understandings of the client's intrapsychic life are derived from the projections and transferences we experience as therapists and, in turn, our own responses to these processes, which is labelled 'counter-transference' (see the companion volume in this series, *The Therapist's Use of Self*). They are powerful events in therapy for both client and therapist, because they are often affect-laden and engage both individuals in an intimate encounter of each participant's internal world.

All the normal responses and distortions of a client's life can be seen in the relationship with the therapist. This clinical relationship becomes an amazing microcosm of the client's patterns and problems (Grant 1997; Grant and Crawley 2000, 2001).

## Promotion of the transference

Within the psychoanalytic therapies, transference and its resolution are considered so central that much of the focus is on creating conditions for the transference to emerge. Thus, the early Freudian notions of therapist neutrality, minimal intervention and no therapist self-disclosure were predicated on creating a 'blank screen' for the intrapsychic projections of the client onto the therapist.

This notion of total therapist impartiality has been replaced in contemporary theorizing with models that emphasize the intersubjectivity of therapist and client. However, there is still an emphasis on promotion of the transference through a variety of means. Gill (1979) argues that the main technique, in addition to the analytic frame itself, is to interpret the allusions to the transference in material that is not overtly about the therapist. Furthermore, he suggests that this is important because the major work in resolution of the transference needs to occur in the here-and-now where both insight about old experiences and the creation of a new experience can occur.

### Working with transference and projection

Psychotherapy is not just a process of talking about events and feelings 'out there' – in the past or in current experiences outside the therapy. It is also a lived experience, where the therapist is a partner in the unfolding of core transference themes within the therapy. Change comes about through re-experiencing and understanding these processes so that new internalized configurations can occur (Bauer and Mills 1994; Grant 1997; Hirsch 1998). This process is referred to as 'working through' or 'working with the transference'.

This process often requires repetition of therapeutic events and interpretations over an extended period. This leads to a fundamental transformation as the interpretations are worked with through the client's fantasies, dreams, responses to the therapist and descriptions of events. Working with or through transference involves exploring and resolving a core issue in the different areas of life where it appears. This can include current relationships, work, family of origin and the transference (Grant 1997; Grant and Crawley 2000, 2001). In non-psychodynamic therapies, this process of applying what is learnt in therapy to other situations is often referred to as 'generalization' (Stern 1998).

### Resistance to transference

Some clients resist the notion that investigating their responses to the therapist is useful and some even deny that they have reactions to the therapist. This is known as 'resistance to the transference'. For example:

> Peter, who has seen his therapist weekly for three years, denies that he has any relationship with her. He tells her that a therapist is like a doctor, and anyone could be sitting in the chair and it would make no difference to him. Once, he took a six-month break from therapy. When his therapist pointed out that the fact that he returned to her was perhaps saying something about the importance of the connection for him, he denied this and said that he couldn't find another therapist.

Resistance can be addressed through interpreting allusions to transference, through examination of historical parallels and through detailed examination of how the client is responding to the therapist in the moment (Bauer and Mills 1994). Such resistance to the transference needs to be distinguished from Freud's early notion of resistance *because* of the transference. He initially felt that the client's transference about the therapist was a way of avoiding the emotionally laden material present in the intrapsychic world.

### Interpretations and transference

The major intervention in working with transference is interpretation or explanation. An interpretation assists the client to understand the latent or symbolic meaning of their thoughts, feelings and actions. The purpose of this intervention is to help the client move to greater levels of self-awareness, which, in turn, reduces internal conflict (Natterson 1986) or promotes internal cohesion (Grant 1997). Interpretations occur in relation to many of the life issues of a client, but primarily address unconscious and conflicted aspects.

The term 'interpretation' is perhaps a little unfortunate. To our modern ear it can sound rather dogmatic or authoritarian – 'here's what you really think or feel!' It is important to remember that an interpretation is the offering of an alternative perspective for the client to consider. Thus, the way an interpretation is made by the therapist is now seen to be as important as the content of the interpretation. A theoretically correct interpretation made in an insensitive manner may not be 'heard' and thus not be therapeutic. Conversely, an interpretation that may not be theoretically correct or sophisticated can, if offered in an empathic manner, still be productive in inviting the client to explore their perception or experience (see the companion volume in this series, *Interventions and Techniques*).

Transference interpretations address the latent meanings of the client-therapist relationship. The therapist 'interprets' the client's feelings towards, and experiences of, the therapist in light of current patterns in the here-and-now and past memories. Transference interpretations are of central importance in psychotherapy; they are the most reliable source for making sense of the client's internal life because they consist of a shared experience that is often affect-laden. Interpretation begins with an empathic understanding of the subjective experience as well as what has had to be repressed, denied or projected. Kernberg (1997) argues that effective interpretation begins with the meanings in the here-and-now and only slowly connects these with the past meanings that have structured the current experiences. For example:

> In working with Daniel's reactions (described at the opening of the chapter), his therapist first carefully explored and interpreted his experience of her in the here-and-now: 'It seems that your disappointment in me has turned into despair that you will never be able to expect your needs for physical care and concern to be met by someone important to you'. Over the next two sessions, this was expanded further to take account of the origins of the feelings: 'It appears that you have experienced severe disappointment in me that is much like the disappointment you experienced as a young child with your mother. Your attempts to get your needs for physical and emotional care fulfilled were not met by responsiveness and you 'gave up', retreated and became depressed. With me, those same needs have been reawakened and you experienced the same despair when your hopes were not met'.

Merton Gill (1982), in a seminal work on transference, suggests that there are three major ways to interpret the transference. *Here-and-now interpretations* focus on the therapeutic situation to help the client learn about and resolve their conflicted patterns of interaction. The therapist may help the client to be aware of other possible interpretations or may note other contrary evidence. These interpretations prepare the way for the client to explore further the origins of their experience. *Contemporary life interpretations* help the client to see that their response to the therapist is like their responses to others in their life. For example, with Daniel, the therapist could have said, 'Perhaps the experience of abandonment and despair you feel in relation to me are the same kind of responses you have to your partner and to your friends when they disappoint you'. *Genetic interpretations* help the client to make connections between their feelings towards the therapist and earlier feelings towards significant figures. The focus is on understanding how these feelings originated in the client's life. These interpretations are frequent in the work of classical analysts, where remembering is considered central to the curative process. Gill (1994) feels that interpretations of transference that connect here-and-now and the past together are likely to be the most productive in promoting change.

Scharff and Scharff (1998) suggest that the best interpretations are short and in an understandable form. When something more complex needs to be said, it is best presented in smaller segments over time. They also argue that sensitive therapists offer interpretations with tact, focusing on the client's experience; this is particularly helpful with clients who are paranoid or distrustful. For example, 'it seems that you feel worried that I will judge you' helps the client to focus on his experience of the therapist and allows him to feel the therapist has some understanding of his inner world.

### Conclusion

Transference is a core process in psychotherapy. It refers to the human capacity to project past experiences with significant figures onto a current relationship with the therapist. The process of transference is not restricted to therapy; it occurs in many of our relationships as we strive to interpret our interpersonal world through the templates established by our earlier experiences with others.

Transference is a particularly potent tool of change in psychotherapy. The therapist can use the transference in the 'living laboratory' of therapy to assist the client to examine and understand their internal world. Conflicts, defences, early patterns of relating become more transparent through understanding the relationship between client and therapist. In this sense, transference becomes a mirror to the self. It reflects the internal world of the client and shows how the client organizes his experience of relationships.

Understanding and being able to work productively with transference is important for therapists of all theoretical persuasions, because transference can create ruptures in the therapeutic relationship that lead to premature termination and unsuccessful therapeutic outcomes.

Transference is not always communicated directly to the therapist. Sometimes there is an allusion to the transference through symbolic means where the client describes interpersonal experiences 'out there' that actually reflect their experience of the therapist. This is technically known as displacement, since the transference relationship, as well as the real relationship, is displaced onto another person outside the therapy, as an indirect means of communicating feelings about the therapist to the therapist (Langs 1992). Transference can also be alluded to in dreams and fantasies, sometimes directly about the therapist and sometimes symbolically alluding to the therapeutic relationship. In addition, transferential patterns may be 'enacted' in the relationship with the therapist, which nudges the therapist into enacting a familiar role from the client's past.

Transference and projection are 'worked through' by exploring the client's responses to the therapist and together trying to understand what the experience is about – both in the current environment of the therapy room and in the client's past and current relationships. Sensitive interpretations of the underlying experiences and feelings offer the client opportunities to understand and change both their internal world and external behaviour. Thus, transference – this mirror to the self – provides clients with a picture of their internal world and how they organize their experiences of relationship with others.

This mirror to the self is not always a simple reflection; at times there are distorted reflections or, alternatively, mirrors reflecting mirrors, which make it difficult to see the original image. The next chapter takes us to such multiple refractions in the complexities of different forms of projection and projective identification, which, more often than not, provide a considerable challenge for even the most experienced therapist.

# Projection and projective identification

## Introduction

Projection is a psychological process that involves the attribution of unacceptable thoughts, feelings, traits or behaviours to others that are characteristic of oneself (Sandler 1989; Clark 1998). Whereas in transference the therapist or others are experienced as having the same attributes as significant others, in projection it is the disowned aspects of self that are 'transferred' onto the other.

In its classic sense, projection is considered a defence mechanism; it helps to protect the individual from a perceived threat and to reduce intolerable anxiety and conflict. Defences reduce the impact of a threatening internal or external experience by moving it from the conscious realm to the unconscious realm (Juni 1997). For example:

> Susan is in an ongoing training group for counsellors. She is often quiet, although at one level she would really like to receive more attention from group members and from the trainer. However, she is vigilant about not taking up too much group time and berates herself if she is the focus of attention for too long. Mary is a lively, extroverted group member; although she is very responsive to others in the group, she is not hesitant to put herself forward for work or to engage the trainer in dialogue about issues relevant to her. During one session, Mary requests feedback about herself and Susan says that she experiences Mary as continually wanting to be the centre of attention and that this leaves little space for others. The trainer is puzzled, because although she finds

Mary a very active group member, she does not experience her as a particularly demanding group member in terms of attention. In a subsequent session, the trainer helps Susan to process what happens for her in relation to Mary. Susan is insightful about her own processes and is able to name her own painful internal reality. She would like to be more central in terms of the group focus, but she continually holds herself back from taking too much space. Susan's feedback is painful to Mary, but she takes it on board and is more thoughtful in subsequent sessions about speaking out too much in the group.

What is happening here? Susan is anxious about the part of her that is like a 'greedy child' wanting all the attention of the mother; she keeps watch over this part of herself to ensure that it does not emerge. Mary, who is very active in the group, becomes a good target for her projection – in this case, the projection is a wish to be more central and receive more attention. However, instead of Susan enacting this part that feels bad to her, she projects it onto Mary and then criticizes her for it. The projection serves two functions: it helps to defend her against the anxiety of exposing this part of herself to the group or to herself and it allows her to blame Mary for taking up too much space and not allowing her enough. Thus, she does not need to deal with her own anxiety about speaking up more – it is Mary who is preventing her from speaking up. This is an unconscious process and it is only through deep reflection and working through that she can begin to own this part of herself. In many cases of projection, particularly in groups, the target of projection is often someone who displays aspects of the behaviour that is being projected. It is true that Mary is outgoing and that she does engage very actively in the process of learning, and thus takes up group time. There is not much in her behaviour, however, that prevents other people from engaging just as actively – and, indeed, some do so.

Projection was first used by Freud to refer to the process of externalizing feelings. One example of this is the externalization of the superego onto someone who is an authority figure; the individual can then play out the internal conflict as an external conflict with the authoritarian or punitive other. Freud later developed the concept as a defence against intolerable internal anxiety. This was particularly in relation to paranoia, but also to phobias. He felt that, in a phobia, an instinctual threat perceived as dangerous could be projected onto external reality where it could be more easily controlled through active avoidance (Sandler 1989). The essence of the defence is the process of attributing repressed contents that are anxiety-provoking onto the external world rather than to oneself. In paranoia, Freud (1911) first identified the role that projection played in creating delusions in the case of Schreber. Schreber was frightened by his homosexual wishes and unconsciously turned his love into a hate of homosexuals. He then attributed this feeling to a persecutory god who hated homosexuals.

Of course, the concept of projection has been part of human understanding at least since Biblical times when Jesus asked, 'Why do you see the speck that is in your brother's eye, but do not notice the log that is in your own eye?' (Matthew 7:3). Projection is also used as a fairly general term to describe any feeling that is external-ized. For example, psychotherapists may use 'projective techniques' that study the internal unconscious states of an individual through what they may project into a picture, object or story. In addition, the notion of infantile projection, where the baby externalizes any kind of tension, is viewed as a normal developmental process (Rafaelsen 1996). Indeed, Freud eventually also enlarged his under-standing of projection to include the notion of projection as a normal psychological trait, influencing the way we construct the inner and outer world.

Revisions of Freud's ideas about projection by Fenichel (1945) are probably more in keeping with contemporary views in personality theory and social psychology. He argues that defence mechanisms, including projection, serve the purpose of protecting self-esteem, rather than that of warding off dangerous sexual or aggressive im-pulses. When the preferred view of self is threatened, the process of projection works to defend the self from the threatening information.

## Projection

Projection, like transference, occurs in all settings; but the family can be a particularly intense site of the unconscious use of this mechan-ism. To begin with, couples often project aspects of themselves onto their partner and much of couple's therapy is concerned with helping partners to withdraw their projections. For example:

> Danielle and Nick have been married for 14 years. Danielle has decided to leave her marriage because of Nick's verbal abuse, occasional physical abuse and obsessive jealously. In

particular, Nick is convinced that Danielle has been involved with other men during their marriage and blames the marital breakdown on this. Danielle has never been involved with another man; indeed, she has been obsessively careful not to even look at another man in Nick's presence, even on TV, because this provokes a violent outburst. Nick is unable to look at his own destructive behaviour in the marriage. Although Nick desperately wants Danielle to return to the relationship, he attempts to do this through coercion; he constantly tells her she is the cause of the marital breakdown and that she needs to ask his forgiveness for her transgressions.

Danielle is the recipient of some pretty powerful projections by her husband. Nick cannot look at his own destructive behaviour in the marriage and he defends against this awareness by projecting the destructive behaviour onto Danielle. She then becomes the destroyer of the relationship. This projection is so powerful and so unconscious for Nick that, although he desperately wants her to come back to the marriage, he is not able to move past his projections to consider changes needed in his own behaviour. To face his own destructiveness in the relationship is too anxiety-provoking and painful for him – so much so that he misses any chance of reconciliation.

Projection among couples can also occur in far less dramatic ways. Traits and qualities such as dependency needs, aggression, ambition, restrictiveness, control or lack of control can all be disowned in the self and projected onto the other partner (Grant 2000). The process of projection interacts with identity processes and gender (Grant and Porter 1994). For example, in couples therapy a male partner may project all of his dependency needs onto his female partner, who he then berates for being 'needy' or dependent. This allows him to distance himself from his own neediness and dependency on his partner and to maintain his masculine identity as autonomous (Grant 2000).

Children also offer enticing opportunities for projections to occur. Parents can project onto children disturbing qualities within themselves. For example, with sexual and aggressive impulses, adolescents become receptive targets of parental projections as the young people struggle to deal with their own emerging impulses.

Babies also provide substantial opportunities for projection. Daniel Stern (1998), in his book on parent–infant psychotherapy, presents a powerful example of how the representations of the mother can be projected onto the child. He describes a mother who experiences her 13-month-old baby as aggressive because of the way he engages in exploratory behaviour with her. She has always seen him in that light and experienced the pregnancy and birth as painful. She is aggressive with him, which, in turn, results in tantrums, more difficult behaviour and further aggression. This mother has a childhood history of repeated hospitalizations and surgical penetrations, which prompted a lifelong vulnerability to physical aggression as a core conflict. The therapeutic focus here was on helping the mother to change her representations and projections about the baby through emotional insight into the origins of her core conflictual difficulties. The baby did not become less 'aggressive'; however, the mother began to interpret his behaviour differently and respond more positively to his self-assertions.

Sometimes sleep disorders and eating disorders in infants are the result of parental projections. Manzano *et al.* (1999) claim that sleep disorders in infants can be connected to a mother who projects a damaged or dead person from her past onto the baby and thus wakes the baby to check on its 'aliveness'. The therapeutic work in these cases does not deal so much with the transference relationship with the therapist; rather, the focus is more on the fantasies and interactions between the mother and child.

## Projection in daily life

Projection occurs frequently in everyday life through jokes and ethnocentric remarks, racism, sexism and homophobia. Strong feelings that are difficult to handle result in forms of hatred towards out-groups or others who are different (Lichtenberg *et al.* 1997). For example, black persons can become the container for those hated inferior aspects of the self; there is then an attempt to control these bad aspects through social and economic domination of this racial group (Timimi 1996). Often these are small-scale comments or jokes, but they invite a response to either collude with the projection or to engage in a fight about it. The difficulty with these smaller projections is that they can create the underlying culture for the acceptance of the more devastating projections involved in oppression, including genocide and war.

Individuals project when they feel uncomfortable about something they experience at an unconscious level within themselves; they may go to great lengths to avoid the awareness of that aspect of themselves. Part of the purpose of projection in groups is to create an in-group who are believed to be free of the disturbing characteristics (Kovel 1992). For example, adolescent gangs project the 'badness' onto other gangs in an attempt to differentiate themselves and feel protected by their in-group.

Critical comments about Aboriginals, sexist jokes about women and derogatory remarks about Asians are relatively common experiences in Australia. These experiences allow individuals to avoid awareness of possessing the characteristics that are projected. The 'otherness' that is created can then be used to help the person establish a sense of distance between self and the disowned parts. The difficulty with this process is that, like all other splitting-off processes, it is only partially successful at keeping the anxiety-provoking material at bay. 'Splitting' is part of the process of projection and is also an allied defence that affords some protection from painful affect (see the companion volume in this series, *Resistance, Barriers and Defences*). Often such views, remarks and actions need to grow increasingly extreme to contain the repressed anxiety. In the film *American Beauty*, this process is powerfully portrayed by the neighbour who is homophobic and who engages in increasingly vitriolic and angry actions to ward off his own disowned homosexual impulses. Killing Lester, the protagonist, is his way of trying to 'kill off' those aspects of himself once he experiences the shame of expressing them.

## Projection in cyberspace

Given the growing importance of relationships on the Internet and therapy provided on the Internet, it is important to look briefly at the potential for projection of parts of oneself in cyberspace. Individuals using the Internet can join discussion groups or support groups, using an alias or a particular persona. It has been argued that such projection of self in cyberspace allows greater exploration and expression of the self; for example, individuals can explore previously hidden aspects of the self by taking on a particular persona (Turkle 1995; Gackenbach 1998). This might involve aspects such as a different sexual orientation, gender, role or personal characteristics. However, although virtual communities can encourage expression of a multiplicity of selves, they do not require coherent expression of self, and the result can be a fragmentation of self or the development of personas that have a very limited and undiversified social range (Reid 1998).

Reid (1998) presents a case study of a virtual self-help group for rape victims where one member took on the persona of a violent attacker and sent abusive, violent messages to the others. Here, the Internet assists in the projective process because of its anonymity; disowned aspects of self are easily projected into personas where the violent, abusive part of the self can function without restriction. Reid (1998) argues that virtual presence lacks the integration provided by the visceral sense of a single self in real life; it severely limits flexibility for negotiation with others because the range of expression is limited.

## Projection in therapy groups

As projection is essentially a social phenomenon, therapy groups provide many opportunities to observe and work with projections. Indeed, the group itself may be treated as an entity for projection of disowned or feared states within the self. For example:

> On the second day of a two-day workshop, the group seems withdrawn and reticent to continue any work at depth. When the therapist inquires 'what is happening here for you that is making it difficult to engage in the work and with each other?', various members begin to talk about the 'lack of safety in the group'. Others mention that the group is too big (at nine members), that they don't meet frequently enough to open up (they meet fortnightly and then for two-day modules of training) and that they have 'done enough of this introspective work'. One person says they trust each individual in the group, but not the group as a whole. Another says that they feel as if the group is judgemental, but can name no interaction that might indicate this.

What is happening here is that members are treating the group as if it is an unsafe entity, and as if they are not a part of the group themselves. Their own judgements of their internal issues and propensity to pathologize such issues have been projected onto the group as a whole, which then becomes unsafe because of the pro- jected judgements. It is only through careful questioning of who and what specifically feels unsafe, that members begin first to process with each other and then to own their own fears of their internal judgement. As one member puts it, 'I've got so much junk inside of me, I feel really crazy when I take a look at it – it's easier to just pretend I don't need to open any of it up'.

It is common in therapy groups for projection to create a scapegoat for the group. Here, group members unconsciously get rid of feelings of vulnerability, failure, weakness and aggression by projecting them onto one group member. The 'scapegoat' is often then subjected to ridicule, criticism or ostracism. Such communicative 'projective identification' (see discussion below) processes coerce the 'scapegoat' into becoming more like the projection (Morgan and Thomas 1996).

Projection is often a highly emotional and intense process for the projector and needs to be treated sensitively by the therapist. Assisting individuals to 'own' their projections is the goal of much therapeutic work. However, since projection is an unconscious process, the client needs to come to this awareness over time. Cognitive explanations about what the client is doing, or confrontations, are rarely helpful and often create further defensiveness. The therapist may need to approach the material in a variety of different ways to assist real understanding in the client. For example:

> In the second meeting of a psychodrama psychotherapy group, Alicia asked for the door to be left open, as the room felt airless to her. Vicki quickly jumped in with a fairly firm 'no! that doesn't feel safe to me, with people wandering past'. Alicia became quite hurt and angry at this response. The therapist explored her experience of the interaction and she said that it felt that her needs were totally unimportant to the group and that Vicki, in particular, had forcefully imposed her will. The therapist empathized with her experience of feeling unimportant in the group and asked her if she had felt this way before. She said, 'yes, that was my experience all the time in my family; my mother was too busy seeing men and drinking alcohol to look after me'. The therapist also inquired whether it was difficult for her to give her own needs priority in her current life. She tearfully responded that that was impossible given the demands of her highly responsible full-time job and her children.
>
> Although this exploration helped Alicia to gain some insight into the strength of her feelings, it did not really 'take the heat' out of her interactions with Vicki. In session 4, Alicia told Vicki that she could see that Vicki was highly critical

of her. When Vicki inquired what gave her that impression, Alicia said, 'it is the way you raised your eyebrow when I said something'. Vicki said she wasn't at all aware of feeling critical towards Alicia and that she had been puzzling about something related to herself rather than responding negatively to Alicia. Again, the therapist empathized with the sad and angry feelings that arise when we feel judged and then processed the event in some detail, with other group members talking about their experiences of feeling judged.

Several other similar events occurred over the ten weeks together. During the ninth session, Alicia was doing some personal work on her family of origin and chose Vicki to play the role of her aunt. Alicia had lived some time with her aunt who had been highly critical of her. During the enactment, she stopped suddenly, looked at Vicki, started to cry and said, 'Oh my god – I know now why I have had such a difficulty with you, I've experienced you like my aunt'.

For Alicia, all of the previous interventions were needed to come to this profound insight about her own projections. Alicia projected her own internal critic onto Vicki. Her internal critic had been partially created through her internalization of her highly judgemental aunt who had been emotionally abusive to her. Alicia also projected her own internal self-deprivation, established through her relationship with her mother, onto both Vicki and the group. These projections needed to be tackled a number of times, by gently exploring the experience, going back to where this experience had occurred before and helping her to disentangle her internal object relations. The rewards of such work are the expanding awareness of the client and the emotional insight that promotes dramatic change. The insight needs to be experienced at an emotional level and the client needs to be ready to become aware of it for true change to occur.

## Projective identification

A particular form of projection is projective identification. First discussed by Melanie Klein, projective identification refers to the unconscious projection of parts of the self (experiences, feelings, functions) *into* and not just *onto* another person (Hinshelwood 1995). The other person is then really believed to have these characteristics and is responded to accordingly. Through interpersonal interaction, the recipient is pressured to identify with the disowned aspects and behave in ways that conform to the ejected feelings and representations. Projective identification moves beyond transference; not only does the client experience the therapist in a distorted way based on past relationships, he exerts pressure so that the therapist begins to experience herself in ways that fit the client's unconscious fantasy (Klein 1946; Ogden 1982). The following example illustrates this process:

Peter (discussed in the previous chapter) often complained that therapy was not working and that he felt more depressed than ever before. He would detail each day and what he had done and how good or bad he had felt. He said that although he had a lot more knowledge about himself, it didn't make much difference to the blackness of his moods, which were linked to how alone he continually felt he was. The therapist found herself over a number of sessions feeling increasingly irritated and annoyed. She also started questioning whether she might need to intervene more actively, given the intransigence of these black, suicidal moods. Her associations were of a whining child who refuses to eat good food that would make him feel better. During one session, the therapist pointed out to him that although he said he had not improved, his detailing of his week indicated that he had felt ok or good for four out of the seven days and that she was interested in what he might make of this, given this was quite different to his experience when he had started therapy. At this point he became agitated and then angry with his therapist. Over time, he was able to tell her that she had denied his feelings and was trying to 'jolly him out of his depression'. It transpired that this was what his mother had done to him continually as a child. He had not been allowed to show his bad feelings and, if he did, she would admonish him for being silly. No-one in his family was allowed bad feelings except his father, who would frequently be angry and brutal.

In this example, Peter has projected his internalized experience of his mother into the therapist. He then behaved in ways towards her that over time generated a set of internal and external responses in her that matched his mother's responses. Indeed, she even had the image of a whining child who will not do what is good for him. Her response was uncharacteristic of the way she would normally work and did indeed deny the deep blackness and torment of his depression when it occurred. The fact that it had come out of an uncharacteristic irritation and annoyance is another clue that projective identification was occurring. One of the hallmarks of the therapist's experience of projective identification is the presence of strong feelings and responses that do not seem to entirely fit with the therapist's self. There is often an experience of being 'out-of-character' or for strong feelings to emerge that don't seem as if they belong entirely to the therapist; in addition, the therapist can feel confused, assaulted, defensive, guilty or paralysed (Foreman 1996; Baker 1997).

Ogden (1982) writes cogently about projective identification. From his perspective, there are three phases to projective identification:

1 There is a wish to get rid of a part of the self that feels threatening or threatened. This is often accompanied by a fantasy of placing the part in another person and then controlling them from within. Thus, there is a significant blurring of boundaries between self and other.
2 The individual interacts with the recipient of the projective fantasy in ways that exert pressure on him to feel and behave in accordance with the fantasy. This occurs through a multitude of interactions between the two.
3 The recipient experiences himself in ways congruent with the projective fantasy. However, because the recipient is different from the projector, there is a possibility that the feelings will be handled differently and hopefully more maturely. It is as if the therapist digests the projection and then offers back a different product that is less pathological. The projector internalizes this through interactions with the recipient, but essentially there are now available some new ways of handling deeply disturbing feelings that had previously been disowned.

This third step in the process can be illustrated through the subsequent period of therapy for Peter:

Much of the therapy with Peter in the period described consisted of working through and understanding in greater detail the impact of the therapist's responses on him. This allowed a different kind of response than he had experienced in this relationship with his mother where bad feelings between them could not be talked about. During one session, the therapist had been quite moved by the depth of his despair and concerned about the possibility of self-harm. In ending the session, she said, with real concern in her voice, 'Hang in there. I'll see you next week'. In the subsequent session, Peter reported that he felt this was the most caring thing she had ever said and that he thought that maybe she had experienced and really understood what it was really like for him. This was the first time in three years of therapy that he had been able to have this experience and he was very moved by it, as was the therapist.

In this period of therapy, there was some containment of both his feelings of anger towards his mother and the feelings of anger that his mother had towards him as a complaining child. These feelings were metabolized as they were discussed and worked through. As this occurred and a different response emerged to his sadness and depression, he was able for the first time to take this in. Indeed, he was able to 'take in' the good food, something he had been unable to really do up until this point. He was able to hear clearly, for the first time, that the therapist was concerned about his potential to self-harm and that she understood and cared about his internal experience.

There is an underlying assumption that what is helpful is the therapist's ability to accept the client's projections, process the projection through a more mature internal structure and then allow the client to internalize the digested projection through their interaction with the therapist (Racker 1957; Searles 1965; Hinshelwood 1999). One of the most important functions is the capacity to transform the distress into an experience of distress tolerated. In the case of Peter above, this was partially the process as he 'took in' the capacity to tolerate the experience of his severely depressed state. The prototype, of course, for this kind of functioning is the infant–mother relationship; here the mother's capacity to both feel the dread of the baby and to retain a balance of mind while doing what is necessary to deal with the distress gets internalized as a containing function (Segal 1975; Hinshelwood 1999).

Like projection, projective identification is an unconscious process. The unconscious wish is that the therapist will be able to deal with the unwanted experience more productively than the client, and that this new model can then be used by the client. This process was first referred to by Bion (1962) as 'containment'. Just as the mother experiences the infant's overwhelming feelings without retaliating or being destroyed by them, the therapist contains the primitive feelings of clients so that they are experienced as more manageable. The therapist metabolizes the experience through a 'thoughtful feelingness' (Baker 1997: 217).

These same phenomena are understood somewhat differently through control mastery theory developed by Joseph Weiss. Weiss expanded Freud's original notion of turning passive into active to explain how clients reproduce traumatic parental behaviour in the relationship with the therapist. They do this by enacting the traumatizing parental behaviour towards the therapist. Whereas in transference they experience the therapist as the parent, the roles are reversed in turning passive into active (Weiss 1993; Foreman 1996). The unconscious purpose is to master the disturbing experience by doing it to the therapist and then watching her response, in order to identify with the therapist's (hopefully) greater strength in dealing with it. There is great overlap here with the notion of projective identification. The difference is that while projective identification is seen as getting rid of unwanted feelings and impulses through their projection into another, control mastery theory sees the phenomenon as a re-enactment of traumatic experience for the purpose of greater mastery over it (Foreman 1996).

## Why is projective identification important?

It is important for all therapists to understand these phenomena, so that they can identify when the processes are occurring and do not internalize them, or become hurt by the client's feelings or injure the client in retaliation. This is particularly so, since there has been a significant increase in clients with borderline and narcissistic disorders presenting for help from counsellors and psychotherapists. These disorders are accompanied by the use of primitive defences such as projection, splitting and projective identification (Glickauf-Hughes 1997). Unless therapists can recognize and deal productively with this phenomenon, they may damage the therapeutic alliance or face impasses and premature terminations of therapy.

Comprehending and being able to work with projections and projective identifications also allows the therapist to reach deeper levels of understanding and therapeutic work. These phenomena allude to internal states that cannot yet be articulated in words by our clients. Projective identification can be a real bridge in communicating such internal experiences to the therapist. Much of the trauma that clients experience is not coded in language, and projective identification allows the therapist to empathically experience important elements of those internal states (Ogden 1982; Baker 1997). As Ogden (1982: 21) states, 'Projective identification is a psychological process that is at once a type of defence, a mode of communication, a primitive form of object relations, and a pathway for psychological change'. If we are not able to read this in our clients, we miss crucial information about them and are not able to fully understand or work with either their internal experience or their interpersonal functioning.

Without an understanding of projective processes, therapists may not know how to manage effectively the intense therapeutic interaction that occurs. Alternatively, they may be induced into colluding with clients or playing a detrimental role (A.J. Clark 1995). Greater understanding of these somewhat ephemeral processes allows therapists to formulate more strategic interventions that can be very powerful in promoting client growth.

## Some principles in working with projective identification

How can we work productively with projective identification when it emerges? The first step is awareness that such a process is occurring. This in itself may take some time, as the therapist attempts to work out what is being evoked in them and where these feelings may belong. It is essential that enough time is taken to truly understand what is going on and this requires the therapist to sit uncomfortably with the projections at times (Ogden 1982; Foreman 1996). Because part of the process involves a form of countertransference, the therapist needs to ask if there are personal issues within themselves that may be producing such strong reactions (see the companion volume in this series, *The Therapist's Use of Self*). Supervision is usually the most helpful place to distinguish countertransference based on the therapist's issues from projective identification that has involved the therapist in a dance that replicates the client's internal object relations. Such a dance can involve parts of the client or roles taken towards the client by mother, father, siblings and other significant figures from the past (Bollas 1987; Baker 1997).

Once there is some clarity about the projective identification, the therapist can begin to offer an interpretation or explanation about what they think might be going on between themselves and the client. It is important here to process the material without acting on the feelings engendered. The projected aspects need to be seen as the best form of communication the client is capable of in this area of functioning, rather than as an attack or manipulation of the therapist. In the end, what is therapeutic is the therapist's capacity to hold the projected aspects without retaliation or withdrawal, because both of these responses will lead to an intensified projective identification. These events can be highly disturbing for the therapist; however, the client needs the material to impact strongly on the therapist to make use of the therapist's ability not to be devastated or paralysed by it (A.J. Clark 1995; Foreman 1996).

Processing of a projective identification looks similar to processing and interpretation of transference. Indeed, Ogden (1982) argues that projective identification is a part of the transference that involves the therapist in enactments of the client's internal objects. As Baker (1997: 219) says:

> Some of the time we may be containers for unacceptable
> affect. Sometimes we are being controlled or harmed by the
> intense rage and desire to destroy the loved object. At times
> we learn what it is 'like' to live our patients' lives; at other
> times, to be the abuser or unavailable, neglecting parent.
> Whatever our role, we can often only truly understand by
> engaging in the dance.

Timing is important in offering an interpretation. If a client is not ready to hear the explanation, he will experience the interpretation as a violent projection back into himself (Marcus 1998). Rather, it needs to be offered carefully as something that is worth thinking about. The process of 'containing' the projective identification is not a passive one. The therapist must be able to engage in an intense relationship, while retaining her function of putting experiences into words. This is dependent on the therapist's emotional and theoretical resources (Rosenfield 1987).

Sometimes clients are not capable of using a verbal explanation or interpretation and instead feel criticized. If this is the case, it is better to hold the interpretation internally and to respond in ways that indicate that the therapist is not damaged by the process. The client will, in any case, respond more powerfully to behaviour and attitude than to words (Foreman 1996; Hinshelwood 1999).

Effective processing of a client's projective identification is dependent on a 'good-enough' therapeutic alliance. With this established, processing may involve challenging distorted and fragmented perceptions, confronting the client with incongruities, and reframing as well as interpretation (Ogden 1982; Kernberg 1987; A.J. Clark 1995).

## Conclusion

Projection and projective identification are powerful psychological processes that occur in families, between couples, in groups as well as in the individual therapeutic relationship. Projection occurs when an individual attributes unacceptable qualities characteristic of themselves to another person; there is then a distancing or judgement of the other person. This process is a defence mechanism, which functions to reduce anxiety about oneself. Working with projection involves exploring sensitively the internal feelings and experiences that have given rise to the projection; then, and over time, the therapist assists clients to 'withdraw' their projections and 'own' more of themselves – including both good and bad aspects.

Projective identification is a form of projection. However, in this case, the 'projector' not only projects intolerable personal characteristics into another, but also engages in such a way with the other so that the recipient is incited to assume the projected behavioural qualities. This is also sometimes called an enactment or turning passive into active. The impact on the therapist is often very disturbing. The therapist can experience strong negative feelings that don't make sense or behave in ways uncharacteristic of themselves. Working with projective identification involves becoming aware of it over time, 'containing' the projection and offering a more 'digested' version of it through an explanation or interpretation back to the client. This requires the therapist to be developmentally mature enough to process confusing and affectively disturbing material.

Understanding both of these processes enables therapists to manage what are often very intense therapeutic exchanges. Without such knowledge, therapists can be susceptible to responding to clients in a collusive, retaliatory or withdrawn manner.

# CHAPTER 3

## Early development of the understanding of transference

### Introduction

We easily lose contact with the origins of our most familiar and widely used theoretical concepts, neither remembering nor appreciating the personal, intellectual and therapeutic struggles from which they emerged. This is true of transference, no less than for other concepts of central importance to our understanding of professional practice.

To go back to the origins of the understanding of transference involves a long journey – long both in time and in culture. The journey takes us to the very different world of the respectable bourgeois society of Vienna a hundred years ago, in the closing years of the eighteenth century and the early years of the nineteenth century. The journey is both important and interesting. It enables us to appreciate in a clearer way both the ubiquitousness of transference and its central role in an evolving appreciation of the centrality of the therapeutic relationship.

In this chapter, we look at the way in which Sigmund Freud discovered – or, initially and perhaps more accurately, experienced – transference phenomena in his clinical work and the ways in which he sought to explain such phenomena and their significance in the emerging therapeutic process of psychoanalysis. We then look at the way in which another seminal figure in the history of psychotherapy, Melanie Klein, introduced a fundamental transformation into psychoanalytic theory and, in doing so, began a process of extending the understanding of transference and countertransference. Chapter 4 continues the story by surveying recent developments in understanding transference, before later chapters look at how transference pheno- mena occur and can be responded to in behavioural and experiential approaches to therapy, and in couples and family therapy.

## Freud's discovery of transference

Freud is often described as one of the handful of people whose thought profoundly impacted the intellectual and cultural life of the twentieth century. Such a description can easily, however, gloss over both the central concerns of Freud's work and the realities of his life – a life that was far from easy.

Freud's early family life was complicated (Gay 1988) and his adult life was not without conflict. From childhood he had to contend with the fact of his Jewish ancestry in an increasingly anti-Semitic culture. The early years of his career involved a struggle to survive, both financially and professionally, as the ideas he was formulating took him down a path that was often controversial (Jones 1964; Clark 1980; Gay 1988; Newton 1995).

Freud was, and still is, both revered and reviled. The influence of his ideas, especially in the field of psychotherapy, is such that it is important to keep the context of his life and work in mind. Intel- lectually, Freud was a product of the scientific and medical culture of the late nineteenth century, as well as of the patriarchal culture of Europe of that era. His biographer Peter Gay (1988) describes how Freud's *Interpretation of Dreams*, one of his most influential works and, indeed, one of the influential books of the twentieth century, was published in November 1899 but had on its title page the date 1900. Gay (1988: 3) comments:

> Whilst on its face this inconsistent bibliographical informa- tion reflects nothing more than a publishing convention, in retrospect it aptly symbolises Freud's intellectual patrimony and eventual influence. His 'dream book', as he liked to call it, was the product of a mind shaped in the nineteenth century, yet it has become the property – cherished, reviled, inescapable – of the twentieth.

Unfortunately, many people, including academics who should know better, discuss Freud's ideas using only secondary sources rather than going back to his original writings. When we read Freud himself, it is clear that his ideas emerged from his clinical work; his methodology was the case study. It is in these case studies that he articulated the experiences that became the basis of his conceptualization of transference and of other key central concepts relating to the functioning of the mind and to the therapeutic process in psychoanalysis.

Freud first encountered the pattern of relationship between doctor and patient that he later came to call transference in 1883, when he heard from his older colleague Breuer about the novel work that Breuer had been undertaking with a patient called 'Anna O'. A physically healthy and intelligent young woman of 21, Anna O was described by Breuer (Freud and Breuer 1955) as 'markedly intelligent, with an astonishingly quick grasp of things and penetrating intuition'. She was given during adolescence to withdrawing into daydreaming, her 'private theatre' – perhaps in response to her 'extremely monotonous existence in her puritanically-minded family'. During the months of nursing her terminally ill father, whom she idolized, Anna O lost her appetite and became physically weak, developed a nervous cough and then a convergent squint. She went on to develop several other distressing physical symptoms that appeared, in the understanding of the time, to be hysterical in origin. Breuer visited Anna O daily and found that encouraging her to talk while in a semi-hypnotic state seemed to result in her symptoms temporarily abating. Anna O called this treatment her 'talking cure' or 'chimney sweeping' (Gay 1988; Appignanesi and Forrester 2000), a process of catharsis in which she recalled memories and powerful emotions that she had not been aware of. Breuer subsequently found that Anna O's specific symptoms could be traced back to various experiences during her father's illness.

The account of Anno O's treatment that was written up by Breuer and published in 1895 (Freud and Breuer 1955) described her as being symptom-free and in good health by 1882, when the treatment ended. We subsequently learn from Freud's correspondence that this was a 'sanitized' version of events, and that the treatment ended for rather interesting reasons. Breuer, it seems, lost his nerve when Anna O reported one day that she was pregnant with his child; the treatment was abandoned forthwith, with Anna O being referred to a colleague of Breuer's and spending some months in a clinic. The pregnancy proved to be another hysterical symptom and there was no suggestion of any improper physical involvement between doctor and patient. Breuer, however, subsequently lost his enthusiasm for the work as a result of this encounter, which would now be recognized as an erotic transference: 'I vowed at the time that I would not go through such an ordeal again' (Gay 1988).

Breuer's collaboration with Freud, although not destined to survive, was of immeasurable importance. Indeed, Freud himself several times acknowledged Breuer's seminal influence in the development of the core ideas of psychoanalysis, especially through the work that he did with Anna O. Not least in importance is the way in which Breuer's experience came to focus Freud's attention on the therapeutic relationship, leading him to see that, in the area of psychological healing, the traditional view of the doctor–patient relationship did not prove sufficient. Thus by 1895, when Breuer's case study of Anna O was finally published, Freud contributed a theoretical chapter to the book in which he described the process of 'transferring onto the figure of the physician the distressing ideas that arise from the content of the analysis' (Freud and Breuer 1955: 390) as constituting one of the three sources of resistance to treatment that must be resolved.

Freud's understanding of transference evolved over time, from initially seeing it as an obstruction to the treatment process to seeing it as an essential component of psychoanalysis. In seeing transference as an obstruction, Freud seems to have viewed a positive transference – feelings of warmth and affection for the therapist, and a wish to please the therapist by cooperating in the method of uncensored free association – as a desirable and even necessary condition for the difficult task of psychoanalysis to take place. Occasionally, however, these positive feelings would either become too strong – as in Breuer's work with Anna O – and result in what Freud termed an 'erotic transference', or else would be replaced by feelings of anger, hatred or blame for the analyst, which Freud termed a 'negative transference'. When the positive transference was replaced by either an erotic or negative transference, Freud saw it as necessary to 'interpret' the transference – that is, to explain to the patient that the feelings they felt for the analyst had their origin in early life experiences rather than in the reality of the treatment occurring in the present. The hope was that such an interpretation would result in a diminution or resolution of the erotic or negative transference, enabling the positive transference to be restored and the real work of psychoanalysis – the 'excavation' of the drama of early life events from the patient's unconscious – to continue. But why were these feelings 'transferred' from the past to the therapist?

A footnote in Freud's 1912 paper, 'The dynamics of transference', provides an evocative starting point for us. He defends himself against the charge that psychoanalysis has focused on 'accidental factors in aetiology' rather than constitutional ones, and continues with the statement that 'Endowment and Chance . . . determine a man's fate – rarely or never one of these alone' (Freud 1912: 97). Thus Freud described the unique combination of circumstances that came to determine the way an individual experiences and expresses the universal need to love and be loved – 'each individual, through the combined operation of his innate disposition and the influences brought to bear upon him during his early years, has acquired a specific method of his own in the conduct of his erotic life' (Freud 1912: 97). This template about love, formed out of early life experiences, determines the way in which all subsequent relationships are approached, especially significant relationships. It is as if, realizing it or not, the individual goes through life asking of every relationship, 'will this be a source of love for me?' For some, the template leads to new experiences, new relationships, being approached positively in the expectation of a 'loving' response. For others, the template leads to the opposite, the expectation of earlier disappointments or hurts being repeated yet again. Freud, still imbued with the biological and scientific ambience of his profession and time, saw this need to be loved as a biologically based drive or force – the libido – that was never fully satisfied and was therefore always seeking new outlets. Thus from the beginning Freud saw transference not as a product of the analytic situation, but as a natural part of life, albeit one that was accentuated and given a particular potency by the unique experience of the analytic situation.

The way the libido found expression in adult life could either be in a relatively mature way, to a certain extent under the person's conscious control, or in a more immature or neurotic way, where the patterns of past difficulties or disappointments were constantly being repeated without any conscious understanding of why this was happening. Here we encounter another key component in Freud's understanding of mental life, 'repetition compulsion'. This term describes the pattern whereby people endlessly repeat patterns of behaviour that were difficult or distressing in earlier life:

> Paul grew up in a family with a brilliant but disturbed father, who always had expectations for Paul that were beyond his reach. His father would also be both unpredictable and frightening in his angry outbursts towards Paul; when these occurred, there was nothing Paul could do except seek to accommodate to his father by being a 'good boy'. With his mother, Paul experienced a great deal of disappointment. She,

too, was in fear of his father's anger, and even though Paul sometimes thought he had an ally in her, she would usually disappoint him when the crunch came – or betray him, as he put it when in therapy as an adult.

Paul presented for therapy in his late thirties seeking help for his chronic inability to sustain a relationship with a woman. Financially successful and attractive, he had no difficulty in meeting potential partners, but the relationships always turned sour after a few weeks. Paul came to realize that he experienced himself as unlovable – his 'template' informed him that if someone got to know him beyond a superficial level, they would be disappointed in him. He would be expected to live up to standards he couldn't meet (as with his father) and would be let down and hurt – betrayed – as he had been by his mother. His life was in various ways a constant unconscious repetition of the painful experience of relationships of his childhood.

Freud's initial hopes about the process of therapeutic change in psychoanalysis proved to be too ambitious: it was not in the end sufficient if he helped his patients recover earlier memories of their life that had been assigned to the unconscious, and then assisted them to understand how these were connected to their present symptoms. Understanding alone did not lead to change. Freud's approach to the transference then changed: no longer was transference an obstacle, an interruption, to the real work of psychoanalysis. Instead, it became the vehicle through which the work was achieved. The clearest illustration of the template acquired in childhood, the template which kept neurotic symptoms in place in the present, was the way in which the template shaped the present relationship between analyst and patient. Thus interpretation of the transference – seeking to understand how the way in which the patient experienced and related to the analyst in the present was shaped by earlier life experiences – moved into the centre of the therapeutic method in Freud's work.

About a year into his therapy, Paul told the therapist that he was going to take a break for several months while he went travelling. He put forward some good reasons for this plan to do with a quiet period in his professional work and his teenage son now being more independent and needing him less. The therapist, however, suggested that this plan – which

Paul was strongly committed to – might be an aspect of the transference. Perhaps Paul was planning to do with the therapist what he did in many other relationships when he started to feel anxious about the strength of his feelings about the other person – he was jilting the therapist before the therapist could jilt him? This lead to the most open discussion that had occurred so far about the way Paul experienced the therapist – the anger that he sometimes felt but could never express, just as he could never let his father see the extent of the anger he felt for him; and his deep fear of finding out as the therapy continued that he was worthless, uninteresting to the therapist, and would be rejected as beyond help, as he had been betrayed by his mother. Paul abandoned his ideas about going travelling, began to demonstrate a deeper level of commitment to the therapy, and started to take the risk of being much more open in his communication about his inner world of hopes, fears and fantasies. More importantly, discussion of the transference became an increasingly important part of the therapeutic work.

As his understanding of the importance of transference developed, Freud grappled with the question as to how the transference could be encouraged in the psychoanalytic process, a far cry from his earlier position of seeing transference as an obstacle to the real work of analysis. From this emerged the belief that the analyst should seek to avoid any gratification of the client's needs or wishes; and the idea was strengthened of the analyst being a neutral 'blank screen' onto which transference feelings could be projected. This ideal of the 'neutral' analyst, which in Freud's own practice seems to have meant the analyst 'keeping a respectful distance so that patients can find their own way, without having the analyst's ideas imposed upon them' (Kahn 1997: 8), appears to have led to the impression that the analyst is unresponsive. This is, however, perhaps more how some analysts have interpreted Freud's ideas for themselves. Freud himself seems to have been much more responsive and interactive with his patients than later stereotypes of the psychoanalyst would suggest (Appignanesi and Forrester 2000). Within the mainstream of classical Freudian psychoanalysis, there occurred a marked shift towards a more structured and impersonal process, to the extent that Freud has been criticized for 'being too real, too much himself with his patients. Psychoanalysis has embraced theoretical notions about transference since Freud's death that are increasingly impersonal' (Thompson 1994: 190). As we see in the next chapter, some recent developments in understanding and using transference are a clear reaction against this stance (Kahn 1997).

## Transference in the work of Melanie Klein

The history of psychoanalytic theory is one of division and factions, a process that has at times led to an introverted absorption with the minutiae of theory. But at other times the tension of struggling with different understandings of clinical material has led to creative developments. One of these developments is the contribution of Melanie Klein to an understanding of the internal world of children and of adults, an understanding that came to have a profound influence on both theory and practice in psychoanalysis and psychodynamic psychotherapy. We consider in particular how her work impacted upon an understanding of transference. In many ways, Klein prepared the way for the developments in understanding of transference which are discussed in the next chapter.

Melanie Klein's life story is both fascinating and tragic (Likierman 2001), although we shall not describe it here. As with Freud, however, it is important to remember that the significant relationships in Klein's life would have influenced not only her theoretical and clinical position, but also the template through which she 'read' the world. For example, her mother, who is depicted as 'an expert in manipulation' (Gomez 1997), was idealized by Melanie. Early in her practice, Klein took on the task, which today would be regarded as highly inappropriate, of analysing her own children. As Sayers (2000) comments, 'now it was Melanie's turn to become the intrusive mother'. Although her daughter Melitta became a psychoanalyst, she was bitterly estranged from her mother and became one of her severest critics.

Klein was always a controversial figure. Her ideas, especially her ideas about the emotional life of infants and children, have appeared to many to be far-fetched and even dangerous. Although followers of Anna Freud in particular have seen Klein as challenging Freud, she saw herself as merely developing what Freud had started. Her work is clearly of seminal importance in the development of psychoanalytic theory, and eventually came to be seen as marking a major point of departure from Freud's work. She sowed the seed for the crucial break with Freud's biological basis for understanding the mind, replacing it with an understanding of the mind that was essentially psychological. In Guntrip's (1971: 47) words, Klein 'is the real turning point in psychoanalytic theory and therapy'. She provides a way of entering the mind of the infant, and of the infant within the child and the adult – 'the archaic underpinnings of adult mental functioning' (Likierman 2001). She opens up the way for a deeper understanding of the complex interplay between the world of internal subjective experience and the external world.

Klein sees the human infant as born with an existing rudimentary ego, a capacity to begin the life-long task of discriminating between internal and external worlds. She describes the infant's emotional life as initially consisting of experiences that were known only in physical terms – primitive and unconscious activity that she termed 'phantasy': phantasy is linked to the language of the body. The body's parts and products are experienced as love, hate, pleasure or poison (Gomez 1997).

Klein describes the progression of the infant's mental life in the crucial first year in terms of two stages, which she named the paranoid-schizoid and the depressive positions. These are not so much *stages* that are moved through and completed, as *positions* – or to use a more contemporary term, *states of mind* – that can re-occur throughout life, especially in times of anxiety or stress.

The paranoid-schizoid position, which, according to Klein, predominates during the first three months or so of life, is marked by the baby coping with the complexity and anxiety of life outside the womb by splitting it into good and bad experiences. There is no middle ground in this position: everything is good *or* bad. Sometimes the good predominates, but at other times the baby 'feels himself to be in the grip of pure evil', or of what Klein termed persecutory anxiety (Gomez 1997). The baby experiences people as 'part objects' – as breasts or penises, for example – and in later life regression to the paranoid-schizoid position leads to people being experienced (through transference and projection) as 'parts' rather than as whole people – as all good, all loving, or as totally bad; for example, as a 'sex object' or 'bread winner', rather than as a person with a range of qualities and experiences. In the paranoid-schizoid position, the concern is survival, bringing order out of chaos, and not worrying too much about the consequences. Primitive defences such as denial and projective identification belong to this position.

In the depressive position, which comes into the foreground from about the age of six to twelve months, the baby comes to a more detailed and accurate picture of the external world. The breast and the mother are one and the same person, and the baby has different and conflicting feelings towards this person. In the depressive position, the baby comes to be both aware of and afraid of his or her anger, with its destructive potential; and feelings of guilt and remorse become concerns, as do means of making reparation.

At the heart of Klein's conflict with Anna Freud in the early 1940s, the 'Controversial Discussions' that came close to splitting the British Psychoanalytical Society, was the issue of transference. More particularly, the dispute centred on Klein's belief that 'the human infant is born with a readiness for social interactions, and so is immediately capable of forming object relations, even though these are rudimentary and incomplete' (Likierman 2001: 55). From this capacity of the child came the ability of the young child to form a transference relationship with the child analyst. Anna Freud, on the other hand, took the orthodox line that it was only in the Oedipal phase that the child internalized representations of the parents, and thus young children had no 'old edition' of love relationships that could be the basis of a transference to an analyst. In response, Klein argued that the young child had already internalized an 'old edition' of love relationships 'composed of the archaic, rudimentary experiences of earliest infancy', and that these archaic internalized experiences were then the basis of the transference that the young child formed. This, she argued, explains why young children have primitive fantasies that idealize ordinary parental affection and make parental disapproval persecutory and threatening (Likierman 2001).

Klein's work has contributed significantly to the understanding of transference and of the processes of projection. She 'widened it [transference] to include not only repressed conflicts but the whole range of earlier emotions which enter into a relationship' (Salzberger-Wittenberg 1970). Klein emphasizes the significance of the very earliest experiences in infancy and early childhood between mother and baby in generating unconscious conflicts, and thus focuses attention on the early mother–child relationship rather than on conflicts generated in the mother–father–child triangle that Freud had described as reaching their peak at 4–8 years of age in the form of the Oedipal situation. From a Kleinian perspective, patients bring into the transference not only earlier conflictual relationships but a whole range of emotional experiences, some quite archaic – the fear of emptiness, abandonment or of destructive rage, for example – that go with those relationships: 'what is transferred are both more grown up elements and all the infantile feeling states which persist right through life' (Salzberger-Wittenberg 1970). For Klein, 'the basic heartbeat of therapy was anxieties and the defences against them, whether paranoid-schizoid or depressive' (Solomon 1995); the therapist's task is therefore to 'hear' the anxiety and the state of mind it activates and to give these experiences form by articulating them.

> Angela had been exploring her early relationship with her mother in therapy. Angela's father had abandoned the family before she was a year old, and her mother had provided everything both financially and emotionally. Her mother had been a very practical, capable woman who was highly regarded by those around her. Angela was full of admiration for her mother's independence and capacity to cope in difficult circumstances. She knew she was loved and that her mother was fiercely attached to her. However, her mother was prone to unpredictable rages that frightened Angela; she described her mother as turning into someone she didn't know, with bulging eyes, long hair swinging around her head, irrational and screaming at her. As a child, Angela had frequent faint and dizzy episodes. In adulthood, she had anxiety attacks, where she felt waves of panic without knowing what was frightening her. Her therapist made connections between the states of fear generated by her mother's violent rages and the current panic attacks. More importantly, however, her therapist 'heard' and was able to fully respond to the state of primitive fear that occurred when the only adult who was available to her turned into a 'witch-like character'. Angela had dealt with this by splitting the 'good mother' off from the 'bad mother' – and a focus of therapy became the integration of these visions of her mother into one whole person.

Klein opened the way for a more thorough psychological understanding of the human mind, including an understanding of how the internal world of object relations that develops through infancy shapes and colours all subsequent interaction with the external world. Her understanding of the constant dynamic interplay between the processes of internalization of the external world and the projection of the internal world onto the external world – for example, the projection of 'bad' feelings onto external objects that are then experienced as persecutory – was crucial. In particular, her work provided a much richer way of understanding the phenomena of projection that Freud had identified, and led to the development of an understanding of the process of projective identification, as described in the last chapter. At a more general level, Klein's work paved the way for later theorists who departed from Freud's biologically based drive theory and developed a relational approach to the understanding of the human mind and of the processes of psychotherapy – developments that are explored more fully in the next chapter.

# CHAPTER **4**

# Developments in understanding transference: psychodynamic psychotherapies

## Introduction

Since Freud first introduced the notion of transference as distortion, there have been a considerable number of developments in understanding and working with transference. As new psychoanalytic theories emerged, they emphasized different aspects of human motivation, which led to very different ways of interpreting the transference. Thus, within the psychoanalytic school, there are many competing theories. Each of these theories has something significant to add to our understanding of human development and therefore to our interventions with clients.

The previous chapter discussed classical Freudian and Kleinian perspectives, usually considered as being underpinned by 'drive theory'. This chapter focuses on three other theoretical developments that have significantly altered the understanding of what is being expressed in the transference: object relations, self psychology and intersubjective approaches to psychodynamic psychotherapy. It also considers brief psychodynamic psychotherapy.

## Object relations

Object relations theory focuses on the centrality of relationships between people and how such relationships are represented internally. The primary motivation for human behaviour is considered to be the seeking of a relationship, first with the primary caretaker and then others. This is distinct from drive theory, where the primary motivation is the discharge of drives, such as libido. 'Object' refers to the representation of another person, while 'part object' refers to the inner representation of a part of a person: this might be a body part such as the baby relating to the breast, or to an aspect of another such as a function they provide – for example, the functions provided by a psychologist or a waiter (Gomez 1997). This focus on 'object seeking' (Fairbairn 1954) assumes that drives, including sexual ones, operate to enable that search (Winnicott 1965; Guntrip 1969). As the baby interacts with others, he or she constructs an internal mental representation, template or 'working model' (Bowlby 1988) about relationships. This includes experiences and expectations about how others will respond, associated effects, and wishes, even defences against relationship – an inner 'representational world' (Sandler and Rosenblatt 1962). Thus, the individual is seen as living out a conscious or unconscious internal drama; they enact roles out of earlier experience, and much of this is, of course, gendered (Grant 2000). New experience is read through the lens of the existing internal dramas rather than experienced fully in its current form (Pine 1990). Thus, while the term 'object relations' sounds rather impersonal and abstract, it actually refers to psychological processes within the individual that go to the very core of the person's experience of themselves and of their relationships with others. These experiences often involve powerful feelings of love, hate, jealousy, rage, yearning and despair (Grant 1997, 2000).

The term 'object relations' actually covers a collection of theories; major contributors include Klein, Fairbairn, Winnicott, Balint, Guntrip, Mahler and Bowlby and, more recently, Kernberg. They all have an emphasis on relationship rather than instinctual drive as the core of psychological functioning. This move away from drive theory and towards object relations theory has shifted the understanding of the transference relationship. The responsiveness or lack of responsiveness of primary caretakers in early childhood began to be considered far more central, and constructs such as the 'facilitating environment' and the 'good-enough mother' (Winnicott 1965) took hold. The importance of good attachment experiences were highlighted by Bowlby (1969) and attachment theory has recently flourished as a theoretical base for several different models of therapy, including constructivism and emotionally focused marital therapy. The capacity to attach is central to transference – without it, the client does not form a therapeutic relationship with the therapist and does not expect the therapist to be able to provide comfort or safety; under such conditions, it is difficult for the drama of transference to be played out.

In psychoanalytic theorizing and practice, there has been a broad shift in the last two decades towards the relational theorists discussed above (Holmes 1998; Mitchell 1999). Such theorists have contributed significantly to our understanding of how early experiences with emotionally significant figures are played out in subsequent relationships, including the relationship with the therapist.

The adult is motivated to repeat early family patterns to gain mastery over them or to gain more security in the attachment pattern (Pine 1990; Gomez 1997). Such patterns are eventually repeated in response to the therapist, and interpretation of the transference focuses on these early patterns (Grant and Crawley 2000, 2001). Thus, object relations sees the self as an internal structure that develops in the context of relationship; the internal structure, in turn, is made up of relationships between different parts of the person or 'internal objects' (Gomez 1997).

### Working with transference in object relations therapy

Object relations therapists understand transference to involve the projection of aspects of early relationships, which have since been internalized, onto the therapist. There is often a focus on early infantile experience and emotion. Transference includes everything that the client brings to the relationship. It is seen as reactivating reactions that were adaptive at an earlier time in protecting the child's self-esteem and making an intolerable situation more tolerable (Gelso and Hayes 1998; Scharff and Scharff 1998). Empirical research is beginning to support the idea that such transference patterns are formed in childhood and enacted in adulthood relationships (Mallinckrodt *et al.* 1995; Andersen and Berk 1998).

Pine (1990) suggests a series of useful clinical questions that are raised by object relations theory in terms of the transference. What is the old relationship that is being repeated here with me? Is the client enacting his or her own role or that of the other? Is the client enacting the person he was or that he wanted to be for his parents? Is this the way his parents wanted him to be? Is this the way he wished his parents had treated him? What early experiences that occurred to him are being repeated actively towards me, the therapist, now?

For example, Angela has been struggling for some months in therapy with issues of differentiation (Grant and Crawley 2001):

*Client:*     It may sound stupid, but I've never had to worry
            about money before and now I'm really worried.
*Therapist:* I notice you refer to your feelings as stupid. Do you
            think that I might feel that such concerns are
            stupid or childish, the way your mother thought
            your concerns were?
*Client:*     Well yes – but it's not affecting your life, but is
            mine. But, this is what I'm upset about, so that's
            ok.
*Therapist:* So it's ok to have a different view and different
            feelings to what you think mine might be?
*Client:*     Yes. Yes it is! Because this is my life – not yours.

In this session, Angela is able to use the interpretation to help her
to move to a more differentiated position in relation to her therapist,
and by implication to her mother. What is repeated here is her early
experience of a mother who was too stressed and overwhelmed to
take account of her ordinary childhood needs. She thus assumes that
the therapist, too, will think she is stupid and childish for raising an
issue that might be important to her, but not (as she imagines) to
the other person.

Analysis of the transference involves the connection of current
feelings and attitudes towards the therapist with early object relations
– both experienced and fantasized. The therapist may be experienced
successively as the cold, withholding mother, the brutal father, the
loving grandma, the abusive older sister. This multidimensional
position is an important part of understanding transference: the
therapist is seldom just one figure from the past, but an amalgam of
internalized object relations. Working through the transferential
relationship leads to internal changes in the client, as they become
more able to internalize what the therapist might offer, rather than
project their own inner world onto the therapist.

Therapy often provides a new object relationship for the client
(Grant 1997; Grant and Crawley 2001). The sustained attention, consistency, non-judgementalness, persistent attempts towards understanding and non-retaliation in the face of client hostility, all provide
a different experience to internalized parental objects. Over time,
this also becomes internalized as part of the client and allows them
to read other relationships differently as well (Fairbairn 1954; Pine
1990; Celani 1993). In Fairbairn's work with borderline personalities,
he argued that, in the first stages of therapy, it did not matter much
how the therapist intervened as long as she stayed benign and

accepting; change would take place over time as the client slowly internalized the new object (Celani 1993).

Because the relationship is so central, 'countertransference' reactions are considered key in helping the therapist to understand the transference. Therapists use their emotions, reactions and associations to the client to enable them to enter the client's world and help to make the transference conscious. Countertransference is seen as an invaluable part of the process that gives a great deal of information about how the client relates to others, rather than as necessarily an indication of unresolved issues in the therapist (for a more comprehensive treatment of countertransference, see the companion volume in this series, *The Therapist's Use of Self*).

Much of the therapeutic work in object relations therapy is focused on the transference–countertransference relationship. The processing of this relationship through interpretations, exploration and what is known as 'working through' (continuously working on the same theme) produces a change in the therapeutic relationship, which, in turn, usually leads to healing of the client's inner world. Part of this process is helping clients to see how they live out their internal world and shape the relationships that currently distress them. For example:

> Terri is constantly angry with her partner because he does not
> provide what she thinks she needs. Terri grew up in a single-
> parent family and her mother had a serious mental illness
> requiring hospitalization on several occasions. Terri learned
> to look after her mother from an early age and to be vigilant
> about her mother's moods. During one session she says to the
> therapist: 'I'm sure you're sick of hearing me come here and
> cry about my life – I feel like I shouldn't come here and do
> that – I shouldn't complain'. The therapist's feelings towards
> Terri are warm and she does not experience Terri as
> continually complaining, but rather as processing her
> concerns so that she can do something about them. The
> therapist begins to get the sense that it's not ok for her to
> have needs, even in therapy, and says: 'It's hard for you
> to acknowledge that you have needs, that you are entitled to
> have needs and to express them, even here with me. At home,
> there was no room for your needs, because your mother's
> needs were so pressing. Here, too, you're afraid that your
> needs will be too much for me'. This interpretation serves as
> a turning point in her capacity to express her needs more

directly to her partner, and allow herself to lean on him sometimes, rather than assuming he would not be able to meet them and then getting enraged with him when he does not provide what she wants. She says that until this moment in therapy she had always 'known' she was entitled to have needs, but had never really believed it. Terri says that there was something in the way the therapist conveyed the message – perhaps in the tone of her voice – which made her know it was OK. She felt calm after that session for several weeks.

Object relations theory contributes a great deal to working with transference, particularly where there are primitive object relations – the all-or-nothing, very emotionally overwhelming subjective experience of relationships – as is usually the case for clients with borderline personality disorders. The client can shift quickly from one part relationship to another, experiencing the therapist as, for example, wonderful or totally disappointing, caring or scornful and dismissive. The task of the therapist is to help the client understand at an affective and cognitive level what they are doing, so they may begin to experience the therapist as a whole object (St. Clair 1986) – a person towards whom they can have a range of different feelings and about whom they can sometimes feel ambivalence (Grant and Crawley 2001).

## Self psychology

Self psychology was developed by Heinz Kohut (1971, 1977, 1984; Siegel 1996), originally to provide more effective interventions for clients with narcissistic disturbances. These clients typically did not do well in classical psychoanalysis. Although a relatively recent development, it has had a significant influence both within the psychoanalytic world and on other models of therapy. Self psychology emphasizes the role of the self as the organizer of subjective experience, the importance of cohesiveness and vitality in self-experience, and the interactional world that structures the self. The 'self' is an elusive concept (Grant and Crawley 2001; see also the companion volume in this series, *The Self and Personality Structure*). Indeed, Kohut himself refuses to give a definition of the self, stating that 'We can describe the various cohesive forms in which the self appears, can demonstrate the general constituents that make up the self . . . and explain their genesis and functions. We can do all that, but we will not know the essence of the self as differentiated from its manifestations' (Kohut 1977: 310–11). Something of the richness of the concept of self can be appreciated from the following description of the self given by Pine (1998: 42–3):

> an ongoing inner subjective state in each of us serves as a filter through which we experience the world – our personal tinted glasses, as it were. Typically these subjective states are organised around worth, continuity, wholeness, and well-being, on one side; around boundaries, realness, agency, and individuality, on another; and around comfort or basic anxiety on yet another. So the tinted glasses through which each of us sees the world may be cheerily golden, denyingly rose-colored, or depressively blue or black; they may be self definingly clear or regressively vague and undifferentiated; or, again, invitingly wide-angled or warily focused. While there may be later routes to such states as well, through conflict and compromise formation, early templates of experience lay down such states uniquely in each of us, so early and so subtly, that they are ordinarily never named or identified. Yet they are likely to affect profoundly both the inner world that is constructed over time and every aspect of the way ongoing life is experienced.

Kohut moves from a model of classical psychoanalysis that emphasizes drives and conflict that need to be unearthed and analysed, to one that emphasizes deficits in the structure and functioning of the self, that need to be empathized with and, in that sense, understood.

Kohut proposes that there are three 'poles' of the core self structure: the *grandiose* sector, the *idealizing* sector and the *twinship* sector. The young child has a set of very powerful needs in each sector that must be responded to in particular ways for normal development to occur. In the grandiose sector, the child has needs for confirming, mirroring and accepting responses and needs to know how important or special he is to significant others. The idealizing sector requires others who can provide safety, stability, wisdom, calmness and strength that the child can merge with to soothe his anxiety and restore a sense of calmness. In the twinship sector, the child needs others who provide a sense that one is like another (Donner 1993; Lynch 1993). Kohut uses the term 'selfobject' to describe how these important functions of significant others are experienced as a part of the self; they supply the needed responses for the self-structure to flourish (Kohut 1984; Lynch 1993). This model of the structure of the self provides a clinical framework that directs the therapist's interventions in working with transference.

*Working with transference in self psychology*

Central to self psychology is the process of empathic immersion into the client's inner world. The experience of 'empathic attunement', over time, allows the unmet selfobject needs to be reactivated. These needs then appear as selfobject transferences to the therapist and take the form of a mirroring transference, an idealizing transference or a twinship transference. If there are deficits in all three sectors of the self, it is not unusual for the three types of transferences to occur over time with the therapist.

This activation and working with the selfobject transference is another central to self psychology. Once activated, the client will unconsciously look to the therapist to provide the missing function from one or more of the three sectors. The therapeutic task then becomes that of fully experiencing and understanding the transference. Once fully experienced in the context of the therapist–client relationship, there is a focus on interpretation through *explanation* (Ornstein 1986; Donner 1993). As in both classical and object relations approaches, interpretation is aimed at tying together the experience in the here-and-now transference with the genetic developmental context of the experience. Such explanatory links help the client to become more accepting and compassionate towards themselves and the deficits caused by an unresponsive family environment.

Such interpretive work tends to be more 'experience near' than other approaches, in that the therapist attempts to stay close to the actual internal experience of the client; the focus is on a spiral of interventions that include acceptance, understanding and explanation of infantile and childhood longings in simple language that the client can understand. This is what is thought to allow their integration into the adult psyche (Ornstein and Ornstein 1985; Ornstein 1986). This bringing together of experiences from different developmental periods in the client's life assists the process of self-cohesion (Grant 1997; Grant and Crawley 2001). Self psychology emphasizes a new kind of experience in the transference relationship where interpretation is only one variable (Baker and Baker 1987). Interpretations tend to focus on the nature of selfobject disruptions, the affects evoked and what the client does to restore a sense of vitality or cohesion.

This means, first, that disturbances to the selfobject tie with the therapist are often the focus of the work and, secondly, that empathic errors made by the therapist are acknowledged and examined for their impact on the client (Grant and Crawley 2001). For example:

> Angela, a 50-year-old public relations consultant, had been in therapy for about two years. She would often ask her therapist for advice about her life. In the early stages of therapy, her therapist redirected these questions back to her. However, it was indicative of her pattern in other relationships, so eventually this was raised with Angela. 'Is it possible that the process occurring between us right now, where you ask me what to do, is similar to the process that occurs between you and your husband and previously between you and your mother?' Angela was tearful in her response, but agreed that this was the case and that it was sad she didn't know what she wanted. Angela, who never missed a session 'forgot' to attend her next session. In the subsequent session, with a great deal of encouragement, she was able to express her disturbance with her therapist and her anger about the interaction. In effect, the therapist had made a therapeutic error by interpreting prematurely and without attending to where Angela was with the material. The acknowledgment and processing of that error led to a great deal of understanding of how such disruptions affected her sense of vitality.

Pine (1990) argues that what is new and corrective is that the client can continually rediscover through the analysis of errors and empathic failures that the therapist remains concerned, well-intentioned and still present. This was an important turning point for Angela. She was able to test the strength of the attachment with the therapist and to experience that the two of them could process these disruptions and understand them, and that the therapist would not abandon or annihilate her if she was upset or angry with her. Indeed, both could survive her negative feelings – something that she had never been able to feel with her mother. Ehrenberg (1992) argues that true change comes from the result of 'new experience in the lived interaction' (p. 23) and that what is significant is not what has happened before, but what has *never* happened before.

Change is thought to occur through the repetition of acceptance, understanding and explanation as new material emerges in the relationship between therapist and client. Over time, the client internalizes aspects of what the therapist does through the process of 'transmuting internalization', until those functions are taken up more fully by the self (Baker and Baker 1987). Such transmuting internalization helps the client to build an alternative stance from which to observe both themselves and others – something that is particularly important for clients with borderline or narcissistic personality disorders. This process is as significant as the insight that comes from explanation and is thought to be central in helping clients to change their inner structure. Working through the transferences consists of completing developmental processes traumatically arrested in childhood (Kohut 1977; St. Clair 1986) and ultimately accepting one's own childhood longings with compassion (Ornstein and Ornstein 1985).

## Intersubjective approaches

Intersubjective approaches have developed in parallel with self psychology and share many of the same basic assumptions. However, such approaches have stretched our understanding of transference in new directions. Transference in the intersubjective approach is seen as an unconscious organizing activity rather than a client distortion:

> The transference is actually a microcosm of the patient's total psychological life, and the analysis of the transference provides a focal point around which the patterns dominating his existence as a whole can be clarified, understood, and thereby transformed. From this perspective, transference is neither a regression to nor a displacement from the past, but rather an expression of the *continuing influence* of organising principles and imagery that crystallised out of the patient's early formative experiences.
> (Stolorow *et al.* 1987: 36)

### Working with transference from an intersubjective perspective

This concept of transference as an organizing activity assumes that the client assimilates the therapeutic relationship into his or her subjective thematic structures. Such a stance also invites a closer examination of the therapist's actions and the meanings these hold for the client (Stolorow 1991, 1997). Thus, the therapist and client are

seen to co-construct a relationship. The focus still remains on how the client experiences the relationship and how the client incorporates the therapist into their subjective world (Stolorow and Lachmann 1984/1985). This tends to create a more collaborative relationship, where the work is focused on the client's experience of the therapist whether or not there are distortions.

As in self psychology, intersubjective approaches also view the selfobject dimension of transference as curative, in that it is often experienced by the client as the 'holding environment' that allows more archaic or difficult material to emerge. Processing of disruptions to this selfobject transference take on a new importance. Such processing allows the ruptures to be mended and permits the arrested developmental process to resume, which leads to more complex organizing structures (Stolorow *et al.* 1987).

The therapist's behaviour must be understood as part of the transference relationship, however active or inactive he or she is. Thus there are two interacting subjectivities in therapy (Kahn 1997; Gelso and Hayes 1998). As in the newer object relations approaches, a great deal of attention is given to countertransference – that is, the organizing principles of the therapist's own psyche. Under the influence of intersubjectivity, the understanding of transference has evolved to take far greater account of the therapist's contributions to the transference and to processing the meaning of that for the client (Stolorow *et al.* 1987). An implication of this stance is that therapists must be non-defensive – they must be open to looking closely at their own activities in the consulting room and understanding their contribution to the client's reactions. This allows the client to then examine his or her own organizing principles.

Peter is exploring his reactions to his previous partner, who he has felt angry with and sad about for the past four years:

*Client:*     I put on the tapes of past skydives to look at – Susan was in them. It didn't chill me the way it normally does. There wasn't the anger that normally comes. There was just pleasure at watching how well we were jumping together. It evoked a lot of good memories.

*Therapist:*  Like you could have good memories without the anger and bad feelings associated with Susan – [with upward voice inflection] yeah?

*Client:*     Yes. I don't know what it is, but when you said that I got really angry – it's so fierce.

*Therapist:* Let's go back to that and try and understand what I did that aroused your anger.

*Client:* It's not what you said, it's how you said it – your voice tone – how it's stretched out. When someone sounds too sympathetic, it gets a reaction. It's like the mocking sympathy we got as children. Praise didn't occur in my family, it was embarrassing to praise someone . . . It's almost like you cannot, you cannot tell me I'm getting better.

*Therapist:* And if I do, what might happen?

*Client:* I get this fierce reaction, like to this guy I know who is antagonistic and is always trying to prove me wrong.

*Therapist:* Does it feel patronizing when I inflect my voice like that?

*Client:* Yes, that's it – it's like patronizing when you overdo the praise or sympathy. And it doesn't take much to do it.

The intersubjective view has raised additional questions about practice. Some writers suggest that such a view implies a greater involvement of the therapist in terms of spontaneity and countertransference disclosure (Mitchell 1991; Ehrenberg 1992; see also the companion volume in this series, *The Therapist's Use of Self*). It is sometimes only through such disclosure that the therapy can breach an impasse. The therapist must be mindful about how such disclosure may impact upon the client and avoid simply re-enacting the client's own maladaptive interpersonal patterns. The therapist needs to ask: 'Am I being drawn into a destructive relationship or is this disclosure going to help the client to move forward?'

These contemporary movements stress the real encounter between two persons making sense of meaning between them. The therapist tries empathically to understand the subjective experience of the client, while offering something of their own personhood.

## Brief psychodynamic psychotherapy

One of the important developments in counselling and psychotherapy in recent years has been the formulation of several models of brief or short-term therapy. There are a number of brief psychodynamic models. Common to all psychodynamic models are the importance of unconscious motivation, the impact of early child-hood on adult functioning and the ubiquity of transference. These models use a time-frame that varies between 12 and 50 sessions. Therapy is typically focused on only one or two aspects of a core pattern that is identified early in the therapy. Thus, it is dependent on the therapist's capacity to identify one pivotal yet circumscribed area on which to focus (Book 1998). The goal of treatment is symptom relief (Crits-Christoph 1992; Luborsky and Crits-Christoph 1998) and limited but substantive character change (Anderson and Lambert 1995).

The briefer models are linked to the longer-term analytic models and can be grouped accordingly. There are those that follow the structural, drive theory of classical Freudian analysis, such as those of Malan (1963), Sifneos (1979) and Davanloo (1978). Here, there is an emphasis on confrontation of defence and Oedipal issues as they emerge early in the transference. There is a group of models that derive from the relational models of analysis, including those of Luborsky and Crits-Christoph (1998), Strupp and Binder (1984), Levenson (1995) and Horowitz *et al.* (1997). These models explore recurrent patterns of interpersonal behaviour that are maladaptive. Then there are models that integrate the four theories of drive, ego, object and self, such as that of James Mann (1973), with an overarching emphasis on exploration of separation-individuation issues.

As we have seen, psychodynamic therapies have placed transference and projection in the centre of the therapeutic process. Contemporary approaches to brief psychodynamic psychotherapy have continued with this focus and have added specific means of identifying and working with interpersonal themes (Crits-Christoph 1998).

*Working with transference in brief psychodynamic therapy*

It is not necessary to detail how each of the different brief psycho-dynamic models conceptualizes and works with transference or projection, some of which treat transference similarly to their long-term origins. What is important to note is that, even in brief therapy, the transference is usually made explicit. By way of illustration, it is worth taking a look at one model that has gained some prominence – the Core Conflictual Relationship Theme method (Book 1998; Luborsky and Crits-Christoph 1998).

The Core Conflictual Relationship Theme (CCRT) represents the central issue in the client's difficulties and is experienced as a core, repetitive, interpersonal concern (Book 1998). It consists of core wishes that the individual has in relation to others, the actual or anticipated responses from others and a subsequent response from self. The goal of the CCRT method, over 16 sessions, is to help clients to actualize their wishes by working through their experience of the response from others as either a transference distortion or repetition compulsion. In a transference distortion, clients may anticipate that both the therapist and others will respond to them in ways that are similar to early significant figures. They might expect that they will be ignored, humiliated, betrayed or abandoned. In a repetition compulsion, the client will behave in ways that engender particular responses from others that conform with previous experiences in interpersonal relationships (Grant 2000). This may entail projection and projective identification.

The example below, taken from *How to Practice Brief Psychodynamic Psychotherapy: The CCRT Method* (Book 1998b: 130–1), illustrates the process of working through the transference with this method.

> Mrs. Benton needed assistance with actualising her wish of being able to put her needs first and to mute her own self-response to deny her wishes. There is a focused approach here of helping her identify her 'responses of others' as transference distortions:
>
> *T:* You began to lose interest . . . when? After I sneezed?
> *C:* Hmmm . . . yeah . . . I think so . . .
> *T:* I sneezed. What did you make of it?
> *C:* Well, it crossed my mind that maybe you were sick. Uh . . . for a split second I wondered if you were coming down with that terrible flu.
> *T:* Go on. Tell me more.
> *C:* I mean, you shouldn't have to be here listening to all my troubles . . . I shouldn't be burdening you with my difficulties . . .
> *T:* You see what's happening?
> *C:* [Quizzically.] I'm not sure. I'm not sure.
> *T:* Well, I sneezed and right away you've closed down. I think what's happening is just what we've been talking about, but now occurring here. You silenced your wish to tell me about this dilemma with that woman because you see me as being sick and therefore burdened and damaged by your concerns.

C: Oh, my goodness! It's that same thing! I worry too much about others and not enough about myself! Like I figure I'm a burden on them! And that's what made me so quiet here: I feared my concerns were too much for you. So I shut up.

The major difference between the working through of transference in brief psychodynamic psychotherapy and longer-term psychodynamic psychotherapy is that the interpretations are kept focused on the identified Core Relationship Conflictual Theme. Like longer-term work, the origins of the CCRT are explored through memories of the family of origin. In this era of economic rationalism, brief psychodynamic methods provide a way of working on one or two core issues at some depth over a relatively short period. Obviously, clients who are functioning well in at least some areas of their life and who are psychologically minded are more suitable for this intensive form of treatment.

## Conclusion

It is useful to think of these different approaches to psychodynamic psychotherapy as each offering a different lens through which to view the transference relationship. The greater number of lenses means that client material is less likely to be interpreted through one narrow perspective. Fred Pine (1990) offers an integrated view of these multiple theories. In a cogent book titled *Drive, Ego, Object, and Self*, he shows how each perspective adds something new to our understanding of human functioning.

It can be seen that object relations enriches the concept of transference through its focus on the primacy of relationships rather than drives. It assumes that the client brings his or her internalized object relations to therapy from the beginning and therefore much of the therapeutic work is focused on the relationship between the client and therapist. Working with the transference means looking closely at how internalized early relationships are being re-experienced or re-created in the consulting room and offering the kind of understanding that assists the client to be able to internalize something different.

Self psychology and intersubjective approaches contribute a vital perspective on transference by helping us to understand how the client experiences the tie to the therapist and how disruptions to that tie could re-evoke disturbances. The self psychology delineation of selfobject transferences into mirroring, idealizing and twinship transferences helped to clarify what important psychological functions the therapist carried for the client. The notion of the self as needing 'cohesion, colour and consistency' helps us to understand how the selfobject transferences contribute to these functions and thus enable the self to be more robust. Intersubjectivity offers a more detailed look at the therapist's contributions to the transference and how empathic errors can lead to disruptions that disturb the client's equilibrium. It differs from self psychology in the way it views the selfobject transferences as only a small subset of the transferences that may be activated. More than other approaches, intersubjectivity emphasizes the concept of transference as the organizing principles that continue to influence interpersonal relationships.

The brief psychodynamic approaches discussed have systematized a process of identifying one or two pivotal themes and then of working exclusively on them through the transferential relationship. They emphasize the ubiquity of transference and therefore its appearance in even brief therapy.

The concept of transference has undergone quite major transformations as these theories have developed to encompass what was being experienced in the consulting room. In essence, there has been a move from viewing transference as distortion to seeing it as a template that organizes incoming information about relationships and thus inevitably shapes responses in the relationship. There has been a concurrent move to investigate the therapist's contribution to the transferential relationship and a growing focus on relational understandings of transference rather than seeing transference in terms of conflicts caused by competing drives. These changes have brought psychodynamic theory closer to other models of therapy in terms of the understanding of what happens in the therapeutic relationship.

# CHAPTER 5

## Schemas and scripts: cognitive-behavioural therapy and transference

### Introduction

Cognitive-behavioural therapies emerged from the behavioural tradition during the early 1970s and have grown to be a powerful force in the therapeutic world. Their central focus is on the empirical demonstration of outcomes, behaviour change and adaptive problem-solving methods. Although there are up to seventeen different cognitive therapies, they share an emphasis on how thoughts are involved in making meaning of events and how this, in turn, influences feelings and behaviour (Dobson and Shaw 1995). Most current cognitive therapies do not view cognition as a unilateral cause of emotion or behaviour; however, there is an underlying assumption that modifying cognitive beliefs, attributions or images is the most effective way to treat psychological disturbances (Beck 1991; D.A. Clark 1995; Rudd and Joiner 1997).

The concept of transference has not been important to either behavioural or cognitive-behavioural models of therapy. However, in the last decade, as cognitive-behavioural therapies have developed interventions to deal with more complex client populations, transference-like phenomena have been identified. Drawing on theories of social cognition and information processing, concepts such as schemas, scripts and interpersonal expectancies have been used to explain how clients interpret and respond to interpersonal situations, including to their therapist. Such concepts bear a striking resemblance to notions of object representations, self-object transferences and working models developed by psychoanalytic clinicians.

## Cognitive-behavioural therapy and the therapeutic relationship

The cornerstone of many therapies is the therapeutic relationship. Until very recently, cognitive-behavioural therapy had little to say about the therapeutic relationship and it has been criticized for its mechanistic and technical view, which has precluded using the relationship as a powerful tool for change (Jacobson 1989; Safran and Segal 1990; Mahoney 1991). Indeed, the original focus for such therapies was on techniques aimed at cognitive restructuring of unipolar depression and anxiety. However, as treatment has been developed for clients with more complex clinical problems, personality disorders or relationship difficulties, the therapeutic relationship has needed to have a much closer focus (Beck *et al.* 1990; Safran and Segal 1990; Kyrios 1998; Sanders and Wills 1999). This is partially because the interpersonal difficulties of such clients make a steady therapeutic alliance harder to achieve and partially because the therapeutic relationship can provide a rich source of understanding about the client.

The 'collaborative relationship' is very central to cognitive therapy. Therefore, difficulties in establishing such a relationship or ruptures in the collaboration need to be attended to before therapy can proceed. When clients are hostile, upset at their therapist or deeply suspicious, it is almost impossible to collaborate in terms of looking together at the cognitions that are maintaining the difficulties.

Recent literature on cognitive therapy with personality disorders has moved the therapeutic relationship to a more central position because of the risk that therapeutic progress will be blocked without such a focus (Beck *et al.* 1990; Linehan and Kehrer 1993; Young 1994). In addition, more recent constructivist approaches, which are a form of cognitive therapy, have begun to acknowledge the importance of the unconscious in producing behaviour (Northcut 1999). Such constructivists talk about 'core ordering processes' (Mahoney 1991) or 'deep structures of self-knowledge' (Guidano 1988) that operate at a 'tacit' or unconscious level.

## Schema and script theory

Although cognitive-behavioural therapists have not focused specifically on the unconscious or transference, they have used the notion of schema from cognitive psychology to describe such processes. A schema is a 'cognitive representation of one's past experiences with situations or people, which eventually serves to assist individuals in constructing their perception of events within that domain' (Goldfried 1995: 55). Schemas are useful for organizing complex material about interpersonal behaviour and direct how we experience ourselves in relation to others and to events.

Schemas develop relatively early in life through our interaction with other people. They can be conscious or unconscious and they include cognition, affect and patterns of behaviour. To this extent, they form a 'template' that acts to produce core organizing principles (Meichenbaum 1995). Thus, schemas guide the organization of new information. Within this model, the therapist focuses on how schemas distort thoughts, create maladaptive emotional episodes or produce unrealistic expectations of self and others (Goldfried 1995; Heller and Northcut 1999). Cognitive therapy helps clients to become aware of and to control the influence of their schemas. Such 'person schemas' appear to be the clinical equivalent of object relations and internal object representations from the psychodynamic therapies.

The client forms a person schema of the therapist that is influenced by the various social schemas already held. For example, because the therapeutic relationship can be construed as an authority relationship, it may evoke schemas associated with parents or teachers (Westen 1991b). Such cognitive-affective processes occur out of conscious awareness. Part of the therapeutic task becomes the examination of these schemas, particularly towards the therapist.

> Jane watches her therapist closely during each session for any hint of a critical response. She has always experienced her father as highly critical of her and, as therapy progresses, she assumes that the therapist too will be critical. During one session she says to her therapist, 'I know you must think that I'm silly and stupid'.

Jane holds a schema about herself that she is silly and stupid and that authority figures will all think that as they get to know her. As therapy progresses, the schema is activated by the asymmetrical therapeutic relationship. This produces fairly strong affect and the therapist and client have to focus on what she is reading into the therapist's verbal and non-verbal responses, which provides her with evidence of this belief. They then have to see who else in her life thought she was silly and stupid and what impact this has on her schemas about herself.

Young (1988, 1994) has identified eighteen distinct schemas that often operate in personality disorders as well as three processes that guide schemas. The processes are schema maintenance, schema avoidance and schema compensation. These are not dissimilar to psychodynamic descriptions of defensive functioning. Particularly in treating borderline personality disorder, there is a focus on 'early maladaptive schemas' (Young 1994) that are the result of disturbed early experience and that lead to a disturbed self-image and problematic interpersonal behaviour. Change in the early maladaptive schemas is required for therapy to be of benefit. Examples of early maladaptive schemas include abandonment, unloveability, dependence, lack of individuality, mistrust, guilt and a fear of losing emotional control (Young 1988).

Other terms in the cognitive therapy literature also refer to this phenomenon. These include 'personal constructs' (Kelly 1955), 'deep structures' and 'tacit beliefs' (Guidano 1987), 'core beliefs' (Mahoney 1991; Beck 1995), and 'irrational beliefs' (Ellis 1994). Beck (1995) differentiates between peripheral and core beliefs and cautions that core beliefs can be difficult to access and to change, because they are often out of awareness.

Another concept used in cognitive-behavioural therapies that is relevant to the activation of transference is 'script'. A script is a schema that involves routinized sequences of behaviour (Schank and Abelson 1977; Westen 1991b). Scripts are used to make sense of social situations and to organize one's behaviour. Scripts are activated in the therapy situation when the client engages in a sequence of behaviours that elicit the familiar response from the therapist that they experience in other relationships.

> Diana has a narcissistic personality disorder. She is frequently angry with people close to her and experiences them continually as ignoring her needs, slighting her and using her. Her continual anger distances people and she then experiences them as rejecting her. During one session, Diana becomes very angry with her therapist and threatens to leave therapy instantly. When the therapist explores her anger and suggests that they take time to terminate if that is what Diana wants, she explodes and says that her therapist is exploiting her. By the end of the session, the therapist feels irritated with Diana's behaviour and finds it somewhat difficult to

restrain herself from acting on this irritation by rejecting the client.

In this situation, as the therapeutic relationship became stronger, it activated the script that Diana used in most of her close relationships. As with others, she became angry with her therapist, attacked and then waited for the elicitation of rejection from her. It was only by processing these events in some detail that the script could be brought into her awareness. By making scripts explicit, the therapist helps the client to examine and change them if they are maladaptive.

Another aspect of schema theory is the notion of 'schema-triggered affect' (Fiske 1982; Westen 1988, 1991b). The client's positive or negative feelings towards the therapist can be seen as the activation of a particular schema or script and its associated affect. This occurs when features of the situation match some of the characteristics of the schema and this triggers the affect of that schema. Here, it is important for the therapist to track the affect back to its origins, where it was attached to a particular category of schema. That category may need to be reworked in therapy if the response appears maladaptive.

A third concept used by cognitive theories that throws light onto transference phenomena is that of 'interpersonal expectancies' (Westen 1988; Beck *et al.* 1990). People carry generalized expectancies of how others, such as men, women or bosses, will respond to them (Grant and Porter 1994; Grant 2000). Such interpersonal expectancies will be used to interpret the therapist's behaviour. The more generalized such expectancies are, the more difficult they are to change, because they emerge repeatedly in the client's life. For example, clients with borderline personality disorder often have quite strong expectancies about being rejected and abandoned by others. Cognitive therapists attempt to find the highest level category for which the expectancy will apply.

In considering transference from an information-processing perspective, Westen (1988) integrates social cognition theory and psychodynamic concepts to indicate some of the cognitive-affective processes that occur when transference is activated. In cognitive therapy models, transference is considered a process that enables assessment and alteration of dysfunctional scripts, schemas and expectancies (Westen 1988; Goldfried 1995). Thus, it is seen as a generalization of the client's pre-existing beliefs and attitudes, especially in the interpersonal arena (Kyrios 1998).

## Transference phenomena as *in vivo* interventions

Cognitive-behavioural therapy typically focuses on content that occurs in the client's life between sessions. Homework, in the form of specific tasks, is often given to complete between sessions. Thus, the focus has traditionally been on extra-therapy relationships and coping skills, rather than the relationship with the therapist. However, cognitive-behavioural therapy has always had a notion of *in vivo* interventions, particularly with phobias. Goldfried (1995) argues that dealing with the transference can be best thought about as *in vivo* work, where the therapist can look at the client's interpersonal behaviour in the moment and work with what emerges between the therapist and client. This here-and-now relationship can be considered a microcosm of the client's problems that can be worked with in the moment (Goldfried 1995; Padesky 1996; Pretzer 1998).

In working with personality disorders, Beck, a central figure in the development of cognitive therapy, has also begun to argue that the interpersonal relationship with the therapist will provide a good picture of the client's relationships outside therapy:

> While this greatly complicates therapy, it also provides the therapist with the opportunity to observe interpersonal problems as they occur, rather than relying primarily on the client's description of the problems, and to use the relationship to challenge the client's preconceptions about others and develop more adaptive interpersonal behaviour.
>
> (Beck *et al.* 1990: 190)

Thus, the emergence of dysfunctional interpersonal behaviours in the therapeutic relationship provides good opportunities for effective interventions because they are active in the moment.

Indeed, Kohlenerg and Tasi (1989, 1991) have argued persuasively for a radical behavioural approach that places a central focus on the therapeutic relationship. They propose that the live relationship with the therapist provides the richest and most accurate source of information about the client's difficulties and that it is also the most salient target for the change process. The language they use is that of behaviourists – operants, respondents, controlling variables and social learning. They speak in terms of the therapist needing to evoke, reinforce, observe and extinguish the client's difficulties during the session and to help the client understand how the past and current environmental contingencies have established the behaviours and cognitions. However, they are promoting a very similar position to psychodynamic therapy, which emphasizes the importance of exploring the transference and helping the client to explore the genetic origins of their object relations.

These recent directions in cognitive-behavioural therapy bring it much closer to other therapies in terms of what is considered central in the therapeutic process. Indeed, Goldfried (1995: 156) states that:

> a consistent principle that emerges across therapeutic orientations is that, wherever possible, it is important to work with events using *in vivo*, affectively charged material . . . Additionally, cognitive-behavior therapists are beginning to recognise that uncovering the historical origins of currently operating negative schemas and relating them to current functioning may enhance cognitive skills and restructuring. Finally, given recent findings in the cognitive literature, behavior therapists are also beginning to recognise the important role of affect in the change process and thus may be more amenable to using such affect-enhancing interventions as the gestalt two-chair technique.

## Cognitive therapy approaches to understanding transference

As the previous section demonstrates, traditional cognitive-behavioural therapy has moved to conceptualizing and working with transference phenomena by utilizing constructs such as schemas, core and tacit beliefs, particularly with personality disorders (Beck *et al.* 1990; Layden *et al.* 1993; Young 1994). Within the cognitive therapy approaches, the constructivists have also begun to stress the significance of emotional and interpersonal relationships in the developmental history of the client (Guidano 1987, 1988; Mahoney 1991). Their treatments focus far more on the 'unconscious knowing processes' and the acquisition of insight in the context of a therapeutic relationship that is safe, contained and intense. Their view is that this facilitates greater depth in exploration of the self and the meanings that people hold about themselves and the world.

There is also a group of integrationists within the cognitive therapy tradition. This group has attempted to integrate some parts of other models to deal with transference phenomena (Safran and Segal 1990; Turner 1993; Goldfried 1995). This group is far more likely to stress unconscious processes, the importance of early development and the uses of the therapeutic relationship. They draw upon psychodynamic approaches and gestalt approaches to work more fully with here-and-now processes in therapy, including transference. Safran and Segal (1990) have enriched cognitive-behavioural approaches by drawing on the work of psychodynamic theorists such as Sullivan, Kiesler and Bowlby to explain interpersonal processes and give direction for treatment. In recent developments of these ideas with narcissistic personality disorders, the therapeutic relationship takes centre stage. Change is seen to occur when the narcissistic schemas are played out within the therapeutic relationship so that they may be articulated, understood and reworked (Peyton and Safran 1998).

However, such efforts at integrating or even introducing psychodynamic concepts like transference into cognitive therapy are not without their critics. Rudd and Joiner (1997) argue vehemently that the use of notions like transference or countertransference violate the principles of cognitive therapy and re-mystify the therapeutic process. They offer the notion of the 'therapeutic belief system', which consists of a diagram of the active beliefs, assumptions, behaviours, compensatory strategies and emotional responses of both client and therapist. The focus is on making the *implicit explicit*, a concept that sounds suspiciously close to the notion of making the unconscious conscious. Although they offer a cogent argument against the importation of dynamic constructs like transference to cognitive therapy, their alternative is a simplistic model that reduces complex transferential phenomena into client roles of victim, collaborator and caretaker and their associated cognitions. Until cognitive therapy can manufacture a more complex understanding of transference phenomena, integration appears to offer the best way forward to deal with such phenomena therapeutically.

## Working with 'transference' in cognitive-behavioural therapy

As we have observed, transference did not receive much attention from the cognitive-behavioural therapies until recently, when the therapeutic methods of cognitive-behavioural therapy were applied to personality disorders. In particular, borderline personality disorders provided a challenge to cognitive therapists, who were accustomed to establishing collaborative relationships with clients that were straightforward and businesslike (Beck *et al.* 1990). Borderline personality disorder clients are known for their intense and changeable emotional reactions, and they are often acutely sensitive to the therapist's responses. This, in turn, can provoke strong emotional responses in the therapist, which can be problematic for those not accustomed to dealing with this population.

The relationship between the therapist and client, therefore, needs to play a much more central role in cognitive-behavioural therapy with borderline personality disorders than with other clients. The relationship needs to be closer and warmer, and the therapist needs to watch carefully for signs of disappointment, anger and frustration directed at them by the client. Beck *et al.* (1990) suggest that it is important to deal with intense emotional reactions directly by first developing a clear understanding of what the client is thinking and feeling and then trying to clear up any misconceptions explicitly. It is also essential to acknowledge therapeutic mistakes and to make it clear that the client will not be rejected by the therapist because of their reactions (Beck *et al.* 1990; Linehan and Kehrer 1993; Sanders and Wills 1999). For example, 'I wonder if part of your anger at me is that I seemed to miss how important your daughter's visit was to you. Does that fit with your experience of our interaction?' The focus in this model when working with borderline clients is to address the underlying issues while working on a series of different problems. Thus, the client–therapist relationship becomes the most powerful tool for changing borderline clients' beliefs about themselves.

Cognitive therapists are directed to be accepting and responsive to borderline clients, with the notion that when clients are accepted as they are, this provides a different experience and thus powerful new evidence about themselves (Beck *et al.* 1990; Linehan and Kehrer 1993; Young 1994). Young (1994) discusses the therapeutic relationship in terms of 're-parenting', where the relationship can be used to challenge well-established schema. In addition, the therapeutic relationship can be used to produce change, by using it as a laboratory for testing beliefs (Padesky 1996) or for learning how to resolve interpersonal difficulties (Safran and Segal 1990). For example, a client who assumes others will always abuse them, can test this out with the therapist in small ways and then observe the results of these 'experiments'. These notions are not dissimilar to the notion of the 'corrective emotional experience' in psychodynamic therapy or to that of 'unconditional positive regard' in humanistic-existential therapy.

Like psychodynamic therapies, cognitive therapy also gives attention to issues of separation and termination. There is a focus on carefully initiating discussion about the client's fears, wishes and expectations in advance of any break in therapy and the importance of preparing clients for termination at least three months in advance (Beck *et al.* 1990).

Whereas previous models of cognitive-behavioural therapy saw difficulties in the therapeutic relationship as problems to be solved before the real work began, current models view problems or ruptures in the therapeutic relationship as good opportunities to assess and work with clients' assumptions about themselves (Beck *et al.* 1990; Safran and Segal 1990). 'What happens in the therapeutic relationship is very likely to mirror the client's psychological make-up and the underlying problems: the core beliefs or schema, and the mechanisms by which the client confirms these schema, are illustrated *in vivo*' (Sanders and Wills 1999: 127). For example, if a client is always late for sessions, there may be a schema about fear of dependency, or a schema about not feeling worthwhile enough for sustained attention. What psychodynamic therapists might consider a 'transference test', cognitive therapists view as schema maintenance. For example, clients will test out the therapist to see if they fit with their own beliefs; if a client believes they are unintelligent, they will seek out responses from the therapist that confirm this.

Within the cognitive-behavioural tradition, Safran and Segal (1990) have been leaders in clearly explicating how to work with the interpersonal processes in cognitive therapy. Drawing on interpersonal psychotherapy principles from the analytic traditions, they emphasize the use of the therapeutic relationship as a place to explore and challenge interpersonal schemas. In working with ruptures to the therapeutic alliance, they advocate taking on the role of participant-observer to avoid getting pulled into the client's 'dysfunctional cognitive-interpersonal cycle' (Safran and Segal 1990). The central process is to be able to observe and participate, much like the 'observing ego' in psychodynamic therapy. Interventions then become a matter of examining in some detail the disturbed feelings and attached cognitions as they emerge in relation to the therapist. For example, the therapist might say, 'When I said that we needed to explore how you often are late for a session, you began to look angry, with your fists clenched. What thoughts were going through your mind at that point?' Alternatively, the therapist might self-disclose some of their experience of the interaction, such as: 'I feel pushed away and kept at a distance by you. Does this fit with anything you're feeling?' This kind of processing also requires the therapist to be skilled at detecting their own subtle feelings and thoughts they experience in response to the client; without this capacity, therapists are likely to stay 'hooked' in the client's inter-personal cycle or make inaccurate assessments of the client's 'cognitive interpersonal schemas' (Safran and Segal 1990). They also emphasize the importance of naming and exploring the therapist's contribution to the interpersonal cycle – much like the self psychology approach of exploring therapeutic errors.

Working with personality disorders can be difficult for the cognitive therapist. When the therapist experiences strong emotional reactions to the client, as in other therapies, it is suggested that they consult with a colleague or supervisor (Beck *et al*. 1990; Linehan and Kehrer 1993). In addition, Beck *et al*. (1990) suggest cognitive techniques, such as the 'dysfunction thought record', to help the therapist gain greater perspective on their reactions.

There has not been a central focus on affect in the cognitive-behavioural therapies. Recently, however, there has been recognition that the cognitive patterns that underlie a particular problem can often only become accessible and amenable to change when the associated affect is present (Strupp 1988; Beck and Weishaar 1989; Safran and Segal 1990). Procedures for stimulating affective arousal, so that there are 'hot cognitions' rather than 'cold cognitions', include role plays, imagery, the Gestalt two-chair technique and working with the client's thoughts and feelings towards the therapist (Safran and Greenberg 1986). Focusing on the here-and-now of the thera-peutic relationship means that the interpersonal schemas are fully activated. It is slowly being accepted that affective experiencing and cognitive understanding need to occur simultaneously for change to be enduring.

## Working with 'projection' in cognitive-behavioural therapy

As cognitive-behavioural therapies have focused on treating the presenting symptoms, rather than the underlying causes or hidden meanings, they have been able to avoid considering how to work with psychological defences (Brewin 1997). However, identified pro-cesses of cognitive distortion such as catastrophizing, magnification and personalization do not fully explain the range of distorting pro-cesses clients use. Nor can they account for underlying motivations. For example, a client resistant to learning and using relaxation train-ing may unconsciously fear being like his father, who he considers lazy (Brewin 1997). An understanding of the use of defences like projection can be helpful here. The client's associations to relaxation may help the more hidden motivations to emerge and these can then be worked with to promote change. In the same way, negative and dysfunctional thoughts may be maintained because they assist the client to avoid facing feared aspects of him or herself.

## Conclusion

Cognitive-behavioural therapy and psychodynamic therapy arose from competing philosophies, methodologies and assumptions about human nature, human motivation and behaviour. They have been at loggerheads ever since in terms of their different perspectives on what works in therapy. However, in the 1990s the two perspectives began to come much closer together with the introduction of schema theory, the acceptance of unconscious cognitive processing by cognitive-behavioural therapists, and the overlaps between social cognition theory and object relations theory.

In developing cognitive-behavioural methods for more complex client populations such as those with personality disorders, theorists have also moved the therapeutic relationship to a more central position. Working with the client's transferences is conceptualized as *in vivo* therapeutic work, where early maladaptive schemas are aroused by the therapeutic relationship. Cognitive restructuring occurs through the 'live' work of processing material between therapist and client.

There is an increasing interest in affect, with the recognition that cognitive change often requires affective arousal. Schemas and scripts are more amenable to transformation when cognitions are 'hot'.

However, it is important not to overemphasize these changes in cognitive therapies. The central focus of the cognitive therapies remains the restructuring of cognitions, self-regulation and behavioural change. Nevertheless, the recognition of aspects of the therapeutic interaction that use different terms, but appear to describe similar phenomena, is surely a significant development for the dialogue between diverse therapeutic approaches.

# C H A P T E R 6

## The real relationship: transference and humanistic-existential/experiential therapies

### Introduction

Humanistic-existential/experiential therapy is a collection of different models and theories that developed somewhat independently. Although therapeutic techniques in the differing models vary considerably, several assumptions are common to all the approaches. These include an emphasis on the 'real' relationship between therapist and client, an emphasis on the whole person including the body, feelings, intellect and soul, a focus on growth, change and development as an ongoing life force, a focus on the capacity for expanded life experiences and consciousness, and an emphasis on the resources and health in the client (Rowan 1992; Wilkins 1999).

Rowan (1983) argues that one of the central differences between humanistic and psychoanalytic psychotherapies is the way transference is regarded and dealt with. Whereas psychoanalytic therapy fosters and works with transference as a way of getting the neurotic issue alive in the therapy room, humanistic therapies have a variety of other ways of working with the here-and-now. Rogerians do this by being constantly attuned to the feelings of the client, whether overt or covert, and focusing on the immediacy of experience in the therapy room. Psychodramatists produce the conflictual event in the present through role-play, as if it is occurring in the here-and-now. Existentialists focus on the task by paying close attention to their own internal responses and working with these responses in relation to the client. Gestaltists get the client to talk directly to the person rather than about them (Rowan 1983).

In many ways, the humanistic-existential therapies were a reaction against the determinism of psychoanalytic approaches and the somewhat technical and mechanistic quality of behavioural approaches. This meant that, in the early phases of development, these therapies eschewed concepts such as transference, projection and projective identification as phenomena produced by analytic methods. Within the last decade, however, there has been a move to integrate these concepts into various humanistic-existential models. Thus, although the focus is primarily on authenticity and the 'real' relationship between client and therapist, there is now acknowledgement that transferential phenomena occur and must be understood and dealt with. This chapter traces such attempts to deal with transference phenomena through five major models within the humanistic-existential/experiential school of psychotherapy: person-centred, existential, experiential, gestalt and psychodrama.

## Person-centred/humanistic approaches

Person-centred/humanistic therapy derives from the principles of therapy established by Carl Rogers. It is essentially interested in the therapeutic conditions needed to create a real and authentic relationship between client and therapist, including empathic understanding, acceptance, unconditional positive regard and congruence (Wilkins 1999). In this sense, person-centred therapists are not so interested in transference. However, their focus on the crucial importance of empathy and the therapeutic relationship aligns them in some ways with self psychology, which emphasizes mirroring and idealizing transferences, which are activated through empathy. For example, Warner (1996) talks about how empathy cures in terms of promoting the reprocessing of experience in person-centred therapy in ways that sound identical to the activation of an idealizing self-object that soothes and calms:

> However, I believe that empathic understanding plays a particularly crucial role in therapy with clients who have suffered empathic failure in childhood to the point that their ability to hold and process experience has been severely compromised . . . The ongoing presence of a soothing, empathic person is often essential to the person's ability to stay connected without feeling overwhelmed.
>
> (Warner 1996: 140)

Carl Rogers advocated a warm receptive relationship with the client. In more recent times, both Heinz Kohut and Merton Gill, from differing psychoanalytic perspectives, started to challenge the notion of the neutral therapist and talk about the importance of human civility and warmth in the therapeutic relationship (Kahn 1997). Although Rogers did not consider the unconscious as central in the therapeutic endeavour, he did emphasize the crucial import-ance of the therapeutic relationship in facilitating change. Rogers, like Kohut, argued that feeling understood by one's therapist was in itself therapeutic and could lead to significant change. In addi-tion, person-centred therapists believe that compassionate accept-ance can be a precondition for the client's self-acceptance. This notion is similar to that of some of the object-relations theorists who argue that clients internalize aspects of their therapist to make new internal object relations in their inner world that are more benign.

Humanistic psychotherapists do not deny that transference occurs, but rather they do not privilege working with the transference over other processes in therapy, and do not see the resolution of transfer-ence as necessarily central to facilitating change (Rowan 1983, 1992). On the other hand, they do focus on the internal responses of the therapist towards the client as a source of understanding the client. They are more likely to self-disclose these countertransferential responses in an attempt to maintain authenticity in the therapeutic relationship. This process of working with the here-and-now relation-ship has only reluctantly been taken up by person-centred therapists. Although it is accepted that the client will repeat his past in the present relationship with the therapist, there is no agreement among such therapists whether this should be given priority. However, as person-centred therapy has moved towards the interactional, there has been a greater emphasis on the here-and-now experiences of the client (van Kessel and Lietaer 1998; Watson *et al.* 1998). Certainly the interpersonal approach within the person-centered model does accept the notion of transference, but suggests that active work with the transference is really only necessary when interpersonal diffi-culties become chronic; they then need to be addressed to create a stronger alliance between client and therapist (Watson *et al.* 1998). For example:

Catriona has been coming to therapy for six months and a lot of progress had been made in addressing her concerns. For the last four sessions, however, Catriona has been withdrawn, sullen and irritable during sessions and has talked about quitting therapy because 'it's not doing any good'.

*Therapist:* It seems something changed about five sessions ago between us and we've had a hard time getting back on track. It feels like you're angry with me about something.

*Client:* No. I'm not angry, it's just that this isn't working.

*Therapist:* You know, we've been exploring how you retreat in your relationship with your partner when you feel hurt and can't get what you want. I wonder if in exploring that you've felt hurt by me – like I'm saying that the relationship difficulties are all your fault.

*Client:* Well, yes, now that you say it like that, I have been feeling like you don't really see what I have to put up with and somehow it becomes all my fault.

*Therapist:* Well that's painful. And I guess that's like your mother always seeing you as the one who was responsible when you and your sister fought. That would make it difficult to feel confident about being open here.

## Existential and experiential approaches

Existential therapy has had a major impact on the humanistic theories, but as a therapy has remained somewhat closer to psychoanalysis (van Deurzen-Smith 1988). Central tenets of existential-experiential approaches include a focus on the person as an experiencing process that is constantly changing, an assumption that the individual can best be understood phenomenologically through the meanings they use to make sense of the world, an assumption that inevitable pain and death are primary to being human and create existential anxiety, and an emphasis on taking responsibility for how we live our lives (Yalom 1980; van Deurzen-Smith 1988; Potash 1994). Key figures in the development of existential therapy include Bugental (1965), Frankl (1969), Yalom (1980), May (1990) and Maslow (1968).

Typically, the existentialists emphasize the development of a real as opposed to a transferential relationship to the therapist, where both client and therapist are touched and changed in significant ways (Yalom 1989; Lantz and Kondrat 1996). Rollo May (1990) has critiqued analytic theory for lacking a concept of the encounter so central to the real or I–Thou relationship. For him, transference 'is to be understood as the distortion of encounter' (May 1990: 55). He feels that psychoanalysis lacks a norm of human encounter and thus has oversimplified the love relationship. Yalom (1980) argues that a singular focus on transference impedes therapy because it prevents the development of an authentic therapist–patient relationship. He also feels that this encourages the therapist to conceal their own self, which interferes with the ability to relate authentically to clients. The capacity to relate deeply to a therapist as a real person is what produces change as the client experiences feelings that have been dissociated for years and moves to an awareness of the love within.

On the other hand, writers like Bugental and McBeath (1995) speak directly about the importance of transference in existential therapy, arguing that the client's 'self-and-world construct system' represents patterns that are inevitably played out with the therapist. This enactment is seen as essential to therapeutic work because these patterns are manifested in the here-and-now:

> Some of the most penetrating and powerful therapeutic work takes place when the client's projections (transference) interact with the therapist's own projections (countertransference) in what may initially be an unconscious collusion. When this hidden conjunction is recognized, brought out into the open, and worked through in the immediate situation, the results can be truly life-changing.
>
> (Bugental and McBeath 1995: 117)

Although there is not the focus on interpretation as a process in the working through, there is an emphasis on tracing the patterns through as many of the client's life venues as possible. It is assumed that the patterns will spontaneously repeat themselves and can be explored for what is valued and what needs to be relinquished.

Experiential therapy developed alongside the existential-humanistic therapies and is closely linked to existential views on personhood and therapy. The essence of the experiential models is based on the two principles of enhancement of the therapeutic relationship and of promotion of the client's experiencing within the session. This is also underpinned by an appreciation of both intrapsychic and interpersonal components of client functioning (Watson *et al.* 1998).

Although experiential therapists take account of the past, there is also a primary focus on behaviour being influenced by the client's vision of the future and a notion that our hopes and expectations affect our memories (Cohn 1989; Elliott and Greenberg 1995).

In addressing transference phenomena, experiential therapists are most interested in specific experiences with the therapist that can provide new awareness. This new awareness, in turn, limits the restrictions of previous emotional schemes through which one interprets experience.

As in the cognitive-behavioural therapies, the challenges of working with the personality disorders have also produced a re-evaluation of the importance of transference and the therapeutic relationship. For example, Potash (1994) proposes that the therapeutic relationship should be deeply nurturing and reparative, so that the client can substitute the therapist for the destructive parental figure. 'A personality disordered patient needs the therapist to function as a good parent while he re-enacts aspects of the entire developmental cycle' (Potash 1994: 142). The focus here is on the therapist providing missing supportive functions that then enables the patient to establish healthier connections with others. This is very similar to the psychoanalyst Fairbairn, who saw the therapeutic process with borderlines as one of internalizing the good object of therapist over time. Indeed, Fairbairn felt that it did not much matter what the therapist did, as long as the therapist was benign and was able to remain so over a sustained period of time; the client would eventually internalize this in ways that changed the internal object relations.

Potash (1994) also discusses the importance of processing the therapeutic relationship. This material is then considered and understood as emerging from learned patterns with parents. However, there appears to be little focus on working directly with the material in detail, or with the possible distortions caused by this reactivation.

More recent writers from existential-experiential therapy have emphasized the therapeutic relationship as an arena for explicit interactional work (Greenberg *et al.* 1998; Rennie 1998; van Kessel and Lietaer 1998). Although labelled somewhat differently, these writers are clearly talking about very similar therapeutic processes to eliciting the transference and working through it. For example, 'reversing the priority between levels of communication' (van Kessel and Lietaer 1998) describes paying attention to the symbolic content of dreams and descriptions of interactional events as providing an underlying reference to the present therapeutic relationship. This process is hard to differentiate from that of psychoanalytic writers like Gill (1982, 1994), who talk about allusion to the transference. Also, the concepts of 'elucidating that interaction pattern' and 'using the therapeutic relationship as a medium for generating change' (van Kessel and Lietaer 1998) are very similar to promoting the transference and working through it. In these processes, the existential-experiential therapist assists a client to begin to understand what they evoke in others and how this has become a familiar repetitive pattern. The therapist makes the link between what happens in the consulting room and what happens in relationships outside and how the client plays an essential part in such patterns. Elucidation of the historical origins of such patterns also help the client to consider whether the interactional pattern is still necessary. Such work allows the client to open him or herself to new experiences with the therapist, thus providing a corrective interpersonal experience (Rennie 1998; van Kessel and Lietaer 1998; Watson *et al.* 1998).

Other relational markers that have begun to be explored by existential-experiential therapists include ruptures in alliances, moments of misunderstanding and shame from lack of therapist attunement, and process identification (Greenberg *et al.* 1998; Rennie 1998). Process identification involves focusing on the current processing activity of the client to help the client increase awareness of their processing. In practice, this looks a lot like using countertransferential material to frame a therapeutic response that describes the client's operating mode.

However, there are also some substantive differences with psychodynamic approaches. For the existential-experiential therapist, working with transference-like phenomena is not necessarily the major process, nor are such phenomena deliberately elicited. There is an assumption that some transference reactions will disappear without working through them, if the working relationship is strong. Such processing does not need to occur with all clients, but is considered most useful in longer-term therapy, particularly with personality-disordered clients or when there are therapeutic impasses. The emphasis, however, is more on the corrective emotional experience than on insight (Gendlin 1968; Gaston *et al.* 1995; van Kessel and Lietaer 1998). In working with the transference, instead of using interpretations, experiential therapists are likely to do something active such as imagining a significant other in a chair and having a dialogue, or going inside oneself to identify and symbolize feelings to be worked through (Greenberg *et al.* 1998). For example:

Jonathon has been exploring how the angry, rebellious part of him comes alive when he deals with anyone in authority and how he always has to prove them wrong.

*Therapist:* Do you experience me as some sort of authority and do you feel the need to also prove me wrong?

*Client:* Yes, I do. I think that's how I sabotage some of this kind of process. I so want to be not suicidal and depressed, but every time I start to feel better, I get angry that you're right about what might help me. I know it sounds crazy – but I do it all the time.

*Therapist:* So are you doing that right now with me? Feeling angry and suspicious and making sure I can't be right about anything?

*Client:* Yes, I am. I'm trying not to, but it just takes me over – this part of me that has to prove you wrong, that is just waiting for the moment I can do that.

*Therapist:* I guess when you say that I think about you as a young boy with your father and how he used to beat you when you did anything that he didn't like. You said that you were angry, but could never say anything because you'd get a worse hiding. I wonder if this part of you has in some ways protected your will – your ability to have your own opinion that is different to your dad's. It was the only way of not having your will crushed.

*Client:* Yes, that all fits – that seems to make a hell of lot of sense for me – it rings lots of bells.

*Therapist:* If you were to put your father in that chair there, what would you like to say to him about all of this?

*Client:* [turns towards empty chair] I don't want to have anything to do with you. You just always had to get your way. I remember on Sundays, all three kids used to have to tiptoe around the house all afternoon so you could have your nap. If we didn't you'd thrash us all. What kind of a weekend was that for kids? Why couldn't you ever think about what we might think or want? It was pretty awful – I remember thinking a lot about death as a kid. [looks sad]

*Therapist:* What would your father say to that?

Client: He'd say I don't know what you're talking about.
I worked hard and provided for my family. It was
just an ordinary family.
Therapist: Was it an 'ordinary' family for you?
Client: No – no. Hell I was scared half the time – scared of
being beaten, scared of being humiliated, laughed
at, made fun of. I don't know where you get your
ideas from [angry now as he turns towards the
empty chair] . . . about what works with kids. It sure
didn't work with me.

The work here with Jonathon is aimed at helping him to express
more directly his anger and need to protect himself from the original object of his feelings – his father. This will hopefully help him
to express his feelings towards his therapist more directly as well,
instead of sabotaging his own progress to prove her wrong. This was
a strategy he used as a child to preserve some sense of inner control
while being brutalized; while it worked then, it is not a helpful way
of dealing with his adult relationships.

Within the existential-experiential traditions, self-disclosure is
also used much less cautiously than in other schools of therapy. For
example, in a case study described by van Kessel and Lietaer (1998),
the therapist immediately self-discloses what she does feel towards
her client when accused of laughing at her in the telling of a painful
story. The therapist then acknowledges that there is something
that gives her that feeling of being ridiculous with sadness and then
gently offers an interpretation that this was how her mother
responded to her sadness. This process is different to the psychodynamic method of exploring carefully first what has happened and
what in the therapist's behaviour precipitated it, before – perhaps –
offering the therapist's experience of the interaction. Thus, there is
less focus on deepening the transferential material and understanding it in all of its facets and far more focus on trying to move the
client back to the 'real' relationship.

## Gestalt therapy

The three main cornerstones of gestalt therapy are field theory, phenomenology and dialogue. Field theory provides a way of thinking about
the whole gestalt of the person; phenomenology provides a process
of defining, working with and increasing the client's awareness;

and dialogue provides the focus on the relationship between therapist and client, with a concentration on the contact and withdrawal process (Yontef 1998; Clarkson 1999). There is a focus on responsibility for self, the here-and-now, authenticity in the I-Thou relationship and on 'experiments' that lead to awareness and wholeness (Harman 1996; Clarkson 1999). The emphasis in therapy is on directed awareness to sensations, feelings and thoughts, so that awareness is developed about how the client organizes their experience.

Although, originally, gestalt therapy was far more interested in the real encounter between therapist and client rather than the transferential relationship, it has moved in the last decade to a far greater focus on the interpersonal world and its distortions (Hycner and Jacobs 1995; Yontef 1998). The emphasis in practice has moved from confrontation and cathartic interventions to one stressing the relationship between therapist and client (Yontef 1997). However, even the originators of gestalt therapy saw an important if somewhat differently understood place of transference in therapy:

> The importance of new conditions in the present was perfectly understood by Freud when he spoke of the inevitable transference of the childhood fixation to the person of the analyst; but the therapeutic meaning of it is not that it is the same old story, but precisely that it is now differently worked through as a present adventure: the analyst is not the same kind of parent. And nothing is more clear, unfortunately, than that certain tensions and blocks cannot be freed unless there is a real environmental change offering new possibilities.
>
> (Perls *et al.* 1969: 234)

Gestalt therapists' emphasis on 'unfinished business' provides a handy container for dealing with transference. They stress how the urgency of unfinished business from the past can be re-enacted in the current client–therapist relationship. As the quote above indicates, the focus is on experimentation in this relationship, which can then lead to change through integration of the more nourishing experiences with the therapist (Heard 1995; Clarkson 1999). The projection of the original 'fixed gestalt' onto the therapist is considered by many gestalt therapists as an important step in understanding the archaic blocks to a full therapeutic relationship based on mutuality. Although transference has a place, the central goal of therapy is a full and complete authentic meeting between two people (Heard 1995).

The 'here-and-now', a catch-cry of gestalt therapy, can be understood as the bridge between the past and the present that allows understanding and change (Harman 1996). The focus on the here-and-now allows the past to live in the present so that completions and change are possible in the transferential relationship. In this vein, how the client relates to the therapist in the here-and-now also then becomes an important site of investigation.

In recent years, attempts have been made to integrate gestalt therapy with some forms of psychoanalysis, which have brought the transferential relationship to a more central position in gestalt therapy (Hycner and Jacobs 1995; Agin and Fodor 1996; Glickauf-Hughes *et al.* 1996). For example, Hycner and Jacobs (1995) integrate intersubjectivity, self psychology and gestalt therapy, showing how there are many similarities between self psychology and most humanistic therapies. Indeed, self psychology can be seen as a bridge between existential-humanistic therapies and psychoanalysis (Kahn 1997).

The intersubjective conception of transference as an organizing activity is a view that fits particularly well with gestalt therapy. This is also true of how intersubjectivity moves the transference into the here-and-now and focuses on how the transference can be triggered by an actual interpersonal event in therapy (Hycner and Jacobs 1995). Self psychology clearly articulates the importance of being experience-near in the transference, a view that conforms to the contemporary focus on being in contact in gestalt therapy. Whereas gestaltists place a greater focus on the actual experiencing of the developmentally arrested ways of being, self psychologists and object-relations therapists are more interested in the meaning of the experience and the developmental picture of the structuralization of self that emerges from it. Gestalt therapy contributes a wider range of techniques for exploration of this structualization through the here-and-now of the therapeutic situation (Hycner and Jacobs 1995; Glickauf-Hughes *et al.* 1996). However, they lack a developmental theory that clearly explains how and when disturbances and arrests occur, an element that is strong in analytic theory.

One of the major differences is, again, the focus on the real meeting between two people. Whereas self psychology focuses on the selfobject transferences, gestalt therapy argues that the therapist must be a person, not just a selfobject and must meet with and engage with the real otherness of another. The emphasis therapeutically is on the mutuality that emerges from a moment of true meeting, even if this happens more so near the end of therapy (Hycner and Jacobs 1995).

*Gestalt therapy, projection and projective identification*

Projection is a key concept in gestalt therapy. It is considered one of the five central processes that leads to avoidance or distortion of awareness or contact. Gestalt therapy emphasizes the owning of disowned thoughts or feelings as part of the pathway towards whole-ness (Lichtenberg *et al.* 1997; Clarkson 1999). Both good and bad can be projected onto others in the gestalt paradigm, and gestaltists work very actively with these projections (Perls 1988; Clarkson 1999). In addition, when gestalt therapists work with dreams, they assume that all the elements in the dream are projections of different parts of the self. Clients are often asked to speak from each element in the first person to assist them in being more aware of that aspect of the self.

Lichtenberg *et al.* (1997), from a gestalt perspective, show how everyday bigotry and prejudice derive from projection. They argue that gestalt techniques will be helpful in 'befriending projecting persons' so that they can become more aware of their projections. Techniques such as calling attention to the relationship between therapist and client, self-disclosing about the impact of the projection on the therapist, and supporting the projecting person in creating a fuller self-definition are helpful in dealing with the disowned parts of self.

An example of gestalt work with projection taken from Glickauf-Hughes *et al.* (1996) is described below:

> One client expressed feeling quite upset about his partner's unhappiness. He believed life would be much better if only his partner were happy. With great intensity, he stated, 'I hate that he's unhappy. It's really hard living with someone who always has such negative energy' . . . The therapist first empathized with the difficulty of living with an unhappy partner, and explored whether his partner's unhappiness made it difficult for him to have his own feelings. The therapist asked if he would be willing to 'act out' his partner's unhappiness in an exaggerated way. As he played this role, the therapist asked the client whether any of those feelings also belonged to him. At this point, he began to acknowledge his own feelings of unhappiness and shame about these feelings. He began to become more cognizant of how he projected these 'shameful feelings' onto his partner. He also realized that while projecting his sad feelings served to suppress his shame, it also prevented him from getting his needs met.
>
> (Glickauf-Hughes *et al.* 1996: 63)

## Psychodrama

Psychodrama is an action method of group psychotherapy developed by Jacob Moreno from the 1920s on. It uses a dramatic format to explore psychological issues and is a powerful experience therapeutically. The therapist is a 'director' who helps the group select a 'protagonist' who will enact a 'drama' about his or her life using other members of the group to enact the roles of significant others in the protagonist's life. It is through psychodramatic enactment of aspects of an individual's life that they are able to use their own spontaneity to deal with past life events or to develop what is needed for the future (Fox 1987; Holmes 1991).

Like other therapists in the humanistic-existential tradition, Moreno was much more interested in the I–Thou 'encounter' between persons, which he labelled 'tele' and described as the mutual encounter of persons based on empathy, than he was in transference (Moreno 1946). Indeed, Moreno was highly critical of analytic forms of therapy, including the notion of transference, and this has had an impact on the development of theory in psychodrama, which stresses encounter, spontaneity, creativity and catharsis (Holmes 1992), but lacks a comprehensive developmental theory. Moreno was more interested in resolving current problems in relationships than in exploring their long past childhood antecedents (Williams 1989) and felt that transference played a very limited part in relationships (Moreno 1946, 1959). He thought that transference was actually the enactment of aspects of roles learnt and internalized in childhood, and that it involved a form of 'role-playing' where the individual enacts roles more appropriate to childhood (Fox 1987; Shaffer 1995).

However, like other forms of humanistic-existential therapy, parts of the psychodrama world have moved more recently towards accepting and working with transferential phenomena in groups as well as the fuller integration of psychodrama with analytic theory (Clayton 1982, personal communication; Holmes 1992). Paul Holmes (1992) provides the most comprehensive attempt to integrate psychodrama and object relations theory. He clearly shows in his delightful book, *The Inner World Outside*, how object relations theory can be used to give a much fuller understanding of the intrapsychic world of clients who participate in psychodrama. Holmes shows how an awareness of transference helps the director to be aware of repressed object relationships that need to be explored on the external psychodramatic stage. Transference responses are multiple in a group setting and can occur in four different ways:

1 In the protagonist's relationship with the director/therapist;
2 In the protagonist's relationships with other group members;
3 Aspects of other group members' relationships with each other and with the director;
4 In the director's reactions to the protagonist and the group.

(Holmes 1992: 48)

In group therapy using an analytic model, the interpretations of the transferences between group members and towards the group therapist are central to the therapeutic work. Indeed, Foulkes (1975) originally called such groups 'transference groups'. However, psychodrama groups encourage far more focus on the 'real' relationship in the present between group members. Awareness or interpretation of transference usually only occurs when interpersonal difficulties emerge in the group that create a therapeutic impasse. Nevertheless, in my experience as a psychodrama director, such transferences are not at all unusual. Psychodrama offers another way of working with interpersonal difficulties that facilitates the discovery and working through of such transferences, often without interpretation from the director. For example:

Eleanor and Sue are in a psychodrama group that is one part of an extended training in counselling. In the previous semester, Sue had strongly challenged both Eleanor and others in the group regarding certain theoretical issues. Eleanor had been wary of Sue ever since, and in the psychodrama group felt very intimidated and frightened of her. She reveals this in her weekly journal, read only by the group therapist. During one session, Eleanor asks to do some work on her relationship with her son's mother-in-law, who she also feels intimidated by. During this work, the therapist asks her how old she feels and she answers that she feels like a 5-year-old with her mother, who was a highly abusive woman. They move to a scene where Eleanor is five and her mother is screaming abuse at her. As a terrified 5-year-old she climbs into a dark cupboard where her mother cannot get at her, but she can carefully watch to see what her mother is doing. Her mother is unpredictable and becomes physically abusive when she gets into one of her rages. This cupboard is one of the few 'safe' places in her childhood memories. As a 5-year-old, she can only keep herself safe by being silent and watching from a dark cupboard. The therapist names her mother's behaviour

as highly abusive, validates her feelings of terror, and asks
Eleanor to use all the strength of herself as an adult to tell her
mother what she thinks of her behaviour and the impact that
it has had on her as a person. This provides a cathartic release
of years of fear and tears and allows her to return to the
present-day scene. Here, she finds her 'adult' voice with her
son's mother-in-law and lets go of the terrified 5-year-old
child. This leads her also to name her fear of Sue and to voice
her concern about the passionate way that Sue approaches
disagreements with others. She is able, herself, to make the
connection between her fear of Sue and her fear of her
mother. With the insight from the drama, she is also able to
move to a new position in relationship to Sue, where she sees
her as a somewhat forceful equal, rather than an intimidating
annihilator.

What is interesting is that Eleanor is able to come to the insight
about her own transferential reaction to Sue, without the therapist's
assistance in helping her to make the connections. The dramatic
enactment of these inner object relations make them clearly visible
to the protagonist. The past does come alive in the here-and-now,
and along with it come alive all of the inner representations of other
people. The template of early interactions is laid out for everyone
to experience, including the protagonist. In psychodrama, this flash
of insight and then profound awareness of the origins of a strong
transference to a group member or to the therapist is not at all
unusual. Indeed, the example given for the section on group therapy
in Chapter 1 describes a similar incident. The beauty of the method
is that it allows people to re-create their inner worlds and experiences from their perspective, and then to observe them, understand
them and choose new ways of being when the old feelings are
reactivated.

Psychodrama is actually a method that lends itself to exploration
of internal object relations. In classical psychodrama, the director
usually begins with a scene in the present; this is often then followed
by a scene from the past – usually the family of origin where the
original interactional pattern emerged. Work in the family of origin
then allows the protagonist to return to the present-day scene with
a different solution to the disturbance. By bringing the protagonist's
inner world onto the stage, with all of its inner wealth, the inner
object relations can be seen clearly, explored and worked with in
ways that promote insight and change.

In individual psychotherapy, the therapist is the only person who is the recipient of transference reactions. In psychodrama, it is as likely to be other group members who are objects of a protagonist's transference. The advantage of the psychodramatic techniques is that, by concretizing the different internal object relations, there is a good degree of clarity and a sense of the tangible in the working through of people's relationships that is harder to achieve in one-to-one therapy (Grant 1989; Clayton 1982, personal communication 2001; Holmes 1992).

On the other hand, intense transferences do occur towards the psychodrama director, although this is often unacknowledged in psychodrama theory and practice (Shaffer 1995). For example, Amy, whose transference leads her to experience the director as critical and controlling, may not be able to express any of these feelings unless there is a focus on exploration of possible transferential feelings. Likewise, John, who identifies with the powerful and all-good director, may not allow himself or any other group member to be aware of any negative feelings towards the director. Psychodrama directors are often pushed into idealized relationships or experienced as authoritarian figures. Such neglected transferences can mask real issues for participants or foster authoritarian relationships, and participants lose the opportunity to learn about unconscious longings in relationships (Kellerman 1985; Shaffer 1995).

Psychodrama offers several ways of working with the transferences within its standard range of techniques. For example, a drama or vignette can be set up that explores the protagonist's experience of the director. This is particularly useful when a group member seems to be resistant or hostile towards the director. Alternatively, the issue can be raised using group sociometry, by asking the participants to place themselves on a continuum, representing how comfortable they feel with raising topics such as 'raising disagreements with the director' (Shaffer 1995). The relationship to the director can be concretized with dyads sculpting each other to symbolize their relationship to the director. And, of course, the issue can be processed directly through verbal engagement and exploration of the relationship between a group member and the director. This requires the director to focus more fully on the participant's experience before moving into a drama that might uncover the origins of such feelings in a family or school setting.

For psychodramatists, an understanding of transference assists the director in knowing where to head therapeutically. It also provides a richer, more varied understanding of the protagonist's relationships and how they are coloured by his internal world (Holmes 1992). The way that psychodrama facilitates the re-experiencing of early family relationships makes it a powerful modality in developing emotional understanding of one's internal object relations. In this sense, it is similar to the dramatic enactment that occurs in the transference in psychoanalytic practice (Holmes 1991; 1992).

## Conclusion

The humanistic-existential therapies, in their early stages of develop-ment, largely focused on the 'real self' and did not view transference as a central part of the therapeutic process. Indeed, the early writers were suspicious of analytic notions and felt that phenomena such as transference or projective identification were the result of analytic methods. However, there have been significant changes in this perspective, particularly over the last decade.

These changes have evolved in the context of emerging psycho-therapy integration. As all models of psychotherapy have struggled with the common and complex problems of the personality disorders, there have been increasing attempts to use the strengths of other models to assist in treatment. Within the humanistic-existential ther-apies, this has occurred at three levels. At the first level, there has been a refocusing on the centrality of the therapeutic relationship in the here-and-now; this has led to awareness of how impasses in the here-and-now therapeutic relationship can impede therapy. Attention has been given to how to work with such impasses that other models might call transference. At the second level, there has been a loosening of the paradigms so that phenomena like transfer-ence and projection can be considered as serious clinical events that must be addressed. This has largely meant either 'importing' the construct and utilizing it without significant changes to the existing model, or renaming it. At the third level, there have been serious attempts to integrate theory and practice from at least two models.

This chapter has traced some of the more thoughtful and clinically astute writers who have been at the leading the edge of such integra-tion. They include Hycner and Jacobs (1995) and Glickhauf-Hughes *et al.* (1996) in gestalt therapy, Holmes (1992) and Clayton (1982) in psychodrama, Greenberg *et al.* (1998) in existential-experiential therapy and Kahn (1997) in humanistic or person-centred therapy. These are exciting developments because they move the whole field forward to a place where the similarities between different models are made more visible while the real differences in theory and practice can be highlighted. In the end, however, it is clients who will benefit from such integration as clinicians become more skilled at a range of interventions that may help them with the often complex difficulties in their lives.

# The transference prism: couples and family therapy

## Introduction

Working conjointly with a couple or family – that is, having both partners or all the family members present in the session – presents the therapist with some unique challenges. Not least of these is the challenge of seeking to listen to and understand, and to actively engage with, two or more individuals *and* the unique patterning, or system, of relationships that has evolved between them, all at the same time. We can add to this the intense and often very heightened emotional reactiveness of partners or family members when their relationships are under stress or threatened. For one of the authors, their very first family therapy session, conducted with a colleague after reading a couple of articles about family therapy in 1971, resulted in two adolescent brothers coming to blows while the therapists and the parents watched helplessly!

Family therapy is a relative newcomer in the psychotherapy field, with its origins usually located in the early 1950s (Shmueil and Clulow 1997; Nichols and Schwartz 2001). Couples therapy, in the form of marriage counselling, has a rather longer history, but until relatively recently lacked a distinct theoretical base (Shmueli and Clulow 1997). Family therapy has been closely associated with what is broadly termed 'systems theory'; indeed, the terms 'family therapy' and 'family systems therapy' were for a while virtually synonymous (Nichols and Schwartz 2001). Systems theory has, however, been an evolving body of knowledge over recent years, and family therapy has made only selective use of concepts drawn from systems theory (for a summary, see Nichols and Schwartz 2001: 104–22). To complicate the picture, the terms 'family system' and 'family systems theory' have been used in some quite different ways by family therapists. For example, Murray Bowen, one of the earliest and seminal theoreticians in family therapy, initially entitled his work 'family systems theory' but then changed it to 'Bowen theory'. Bowen's reasoning was that his understanding of the nature of family systems was markedly different to that derived by other family therapists who drew from the body of knowledge known as 'general systems theory' (Kerr and Bowen 1988). Despite the subtleties and complexities of its usage, however, the notion of 'family system' is the central concept in family therapy; it also points us to an important difference between family therapy and other modalities of psychotherapy about the ways in which they understand the therapeutic process.

Before the emergence of family therapy as a therapeutic modality in the early 1950s, there was a growing concern about existing ways of conceiving of emotional and psychiatric problems as residing exclusively within the individual patient, rather than being influenced by – or even being a product of – the individual's network of relationships. Family therapy both articulated this concern and provided a vehicle by which the relationship matrix of which the individual was a part could be helped to change. Expressed at the most simple level, if this relational matrix changed, then the individual's symptoms would become redundant. From today's vantage point, it is sometimes difficult to see how radical such ideas were thirty or more years ago.

Many of the early pioneers of family therapy – Murray Bowen, Nathan Ackerman, Don Jackson, Salvadore Minuchin, Mara Selvini Palazzoli – were originally trained in psychoanalysis. Mostly, however, they came to reject this as a way of conceptualizing and practising psychotherapy. Their way of thinking about emotional and psychiatric problems and about therapy – their epistemology – was often seen as a radical departure from psychoanalysis, and concepts drawn from the two approaches were seen as incompatible. One of the negative consequences of adopting a dogmatic emphasis on viewing people's problems from only a systemic perspective has often been an undervaluing, or ignoring, by family therapists of the internal world of subjective experience of partners or family members, a subjectivity that is at the core of the meaning people attribute to their experiences in relationships, and which can therefore greatly influence the pattern of interaction in a particular relationship system (Nichols 1987). In recent years, the divide between systemic and psychodynamic approaches to relationships has been questioned by a growing number of family therapists (Nichols 1987; Dallos and Draper 2000), and psychodynamic ideas are being re-examined, even by those family therapists who initially eschewed them (Flaskas and Perlesz 1996). In this process, an understanding of the importance of 'meaning' is proving to be a bridge between the psychodynamic and systemic traditions.

We must also acknowledge that not all family and couples therapists rejected a psychodynamic understanding of relationships. There has been a strong and continuing tradition of a psychodynamic approach to family and couples therapy (Skynner 1976; Stierlin 1977; Slipp 1981, 1984; Scharff and Scharff 1987, 1991), even when mainstream family therapy was fiercely anti-psychoanalytic (Nichols and Schwartz 2001). Couples therapy, often subsumed into family therapy but increasingly emerging as a therapeutic modality in its own right, has also maintained a vigorous psychodynamic understanding of therapy alongside more systemic approaches (Dicks 1967; Clulow and Mattinson 1989; Solomon 1989; Siegel 1992; Shaddock 2000; Clulow 2001). One explanation for this difference in use of theory may be that the concerns that couples bring to therapy are often less pragmatic than those presented by families, with issues such as intimacy, trust or the pain of the threatened loss of the relationship requiring that subjective experience be given centre stage.

Patterns of couple and family interaction are highly complex and often fast-moving. The more we seek to understand them, the more we realize that many of the descriptive frameworks we draw upon are actually only simplifications of this highly complex reality. When we think we have a moment of illumination, our understanding often seems to end up being transitory and limited. This complexity is, of course, part of what makes relationship therapy such a fascinating and potentially rewarding form of clinical practice. This chaotic confusion, which is often so central to intimate relationships that are in difficulty, can only start to make sense when we think in terms of the well-established web of transferences and projections that exist between the partners. Indeed, the confusion itself is often telling us something important about the hopes, fears and hurts of the parties to the relationship if only we can help them to begin to untangle its meaning at a less conscious level.

Gary and Diane had been emotionally distant and estranged in their relationship for several years, more than once at the point of separation. In therapy, over the space of about

18 months, they had each been able to work through some
painful individual issues, and appeared to be at the point
of tentatively moving towards a more open and intimate
relationship with each other. They then came to a session
reporting a bitter fight: 'all the therapy has been pointless'
was the only thing they could agree upon as the session
progressed! Yet the therapist's initial disappointment and
anxiety gradually gave way to a realization that they had in
fact taken a huge step forward. In allowing themselves to
express so much hurt and anger so directly to each other they
were engaging more intimately than they had for a long
time. This had profound implications for the conduct of the
session: their row was cause for celebration rather than
problem-solving!

Even though the unique nature of the therapeutic relationship,
in any modality of therapy, may often bring patterns of transference
or projection into the foreground of the relationship of client and
therapist, the phenomenon of transference is not one that belongs
exclusively to the therapeutic realm. The essence of transference, as
we have discussed, is that early developmental experiences give the
individual a template – or, in Bowlby's (1969, 1988) helpful phrase,
an 'internal working model' – through which meaning is attached
to later relationship experiences. The more significant the relationship, the more likely it is that the person will, unconsciously, resort
to their own unique template of earlier experiences to manage the
current relationship situation – to make sense of their own experiences
in the relationship, to provide an explanation for what they perceive
to be the other's experience and behaviour in the relationship, and
thus to guide their own future behaviour in the relationship. And,
of course, our relationships with our partners, our children and our
parents (or our internalized memories of our parents) are among our
most emotionally significant relationships as adults.

Couple and family relationships are, therefore, an amalgam of
transference and of reality. Or, to use a more contemporary intersubjective understanding of transference, our experience of our
relationships with family members will be the result of a complex
process of co-construction of the relationship, where an important
ingredient is the template each takes into the relationship process
from earlier relationship experiences.

This chapter outlines some of the ways in which the concepts of
transference and projection can assist the therapist working with

couple or family relationships. To make a large topic more manageable, we look at it in three ways:

- Ways in which these concepts can assist the therapist in making sense of the patterns and dynamics of couple and family relationships.
- Ways in which an understanding of transference and projection can illuminate aspects of what happens in the therapeutic relationship in couples and family therapy.
- Ways in which an understanding of transference and projection can inform interventions aimed at modifying the patterns of relationships in couples and family therapy.

## Understanding couple and family relationships

Each of us has our own unique repertoire of relationship experiences, beginning with the very earliest experiences with our mother and other care-givers when we were babies. Some of these experiences were what we needed at the time – 'good enough' experiences, in Winnicott's (1965) memorable phrase – to facilitate our development, whereas others were disappointing or even absent, or perhaps too overwhelming in terms of the excitement or frustration involved. From this repertoire of early life experiences, each of us develops our own unconscious 'agenda for relationship', the uniquely personal pattern of what we look for, expect, fear and long for in our adult relationships. This becomes our personal template through which we instinctively, and largely unconsciously, manage our experience of relationships. It thus also becomes the source of our transference responses and projections, both to people who are at the moment significant in our lives and to specific events within those relationships.

One dimension of this process of establishing an agenda or template for relationship, through which current relationships are experienced, is receiving increasing attention in the couples therapy literature. This is the individual's pattern of adult attachment and the ways in which this impacts on the couple relationship. Bowlby (1988) uses the term 'internal working model' to describe the individual's pattern of attachment behaviour, the way in which the person responds to a real or perceived threat to security. Bowlby's own work and later work by other researchers (Bretherton 1991) suggests that the working model acquired in early childhood, although capable

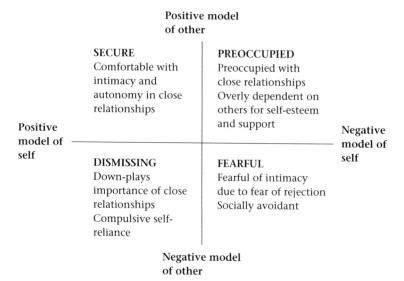

**Positive model
of other**

| SECURE | PREOCCUPIED |
|---|---|
| Comfortable with intimacy and autonomy in close relationships | Preoccupied with close relationships Overly dependent on others for self-esteem and support |

**Positive model of self** ——————————————— **Negative model of self**

| DISMISSING | FEARFUL |
|---|---|
| Down-plays importance of close relationships Compulsive self-reliance | Fearful of intimacy due to fear of rejection Socially avoidant |

**Negative model
of other**

**Figure 7.1** Two-dimensional, four-category model of adult attachment (reproduced from Bartholomew, Henderson and Dutton 2001).

of modification under the impact of later life experiences, continues through into adult life. Bartholomew *et al.* (2001) provide a helpful framework for thinking about the various forms that adult attachment behaviour can take. Based on two underlying dimensions of 'positivity of the self' and 'positivity of the other', they suggest four quadrants that represent the four commonly identified patterns of adult attachment (see Figure 7.1).

A person's agenda for relationship plays a significant role in the process of choosing a partner. In the book co-authored by John Cleese and pioneering family therapist Robin Skynner (Skynner and Cleese 1984), there is a telling illustration of unconscious processes of attraction at work. Skynner describes to Cleese a process of asking participants in a family therapy training workshop, while still strangers to each other, to choose someone else in the group who makes them think of someone in their own family of origin, or who could perhaps fill a 'gap' in their family. This exercise is conducted without any verbal interaction. When everyone is paired off, they are asked to talk together as a couple to see what brought them together. Each pair is then asked to choose another pair, and the resulting foursome is asked to create a role-play family. Then they are asked to talk about what aspects of their family backgrounds led them to make their decisions about roles in the family they have just created. The results are fascinating. Skynner describes how the workshop participants frequently end up with others whose family of origin functioned or functions in a similar way to their own. All four might come from a family where there has been difficulty in sharing affection, or managing anger or envy, or where there has been an expectation that everyone will be cheerful and positive all the time. Or there might have been a similar absence of a parent, or a shared experience of loss or change in the family. Initially, Skynner was anxious about those participants who were the last to choose partners in the exercise – the 'wall-flowers' – whom he feared might feel rejected. In his anxiety, he put off asking these people about their experience until last, rather dreading what their response might be. Their experience was the same as for others, however; they discovered that they, too, had found partners with whom they shared family of origin themes, all sharing in some way the experience of being rejected early in their lives.

Dicks (1967) describes the process of choosing a marital partner that involves three levels of choice. To paraphrase Dicks, first social and cultural factors, along with the circumstances of our lives, define a population field within which a partner is likely to be found. Second, within this parameter, there is a conscious process of choosing someone, based on personal values, shared interests, physical attraction, and so on. Third, there are the unconscious forces, the 'chemistry', based upon the object relations (the positive and negative elements of the agenda for relationship) of each partner. There appears to be an exquisitely accurate unconscious process that identifies a partner who will fit with our particular agenda for relationship. Sometimes this 'fit' is to do with our unconscious need for a second opportunity to resolve difficulties we could not resolve at an earlier developmental stage; at other times, it seems more to do with finding someone onto whom we can project – and then identify with – disowned aspects of our own personality:

> Anthony and Mary came together as a couple when each was in their early thirties; both already had a history of relationships that had not worked out, and it appeared that this was to be yet another disappointment for them. Their relationship was characterized by repeated angry outbursts from Mary, usually when she felt Anthony was being emotionally absent from the relationship, followed by a

period of separation. Yet they seemed reluctant to part, despite the difficulties.

Mary grew up in a family where she was the eldest of three siblings. The middle sibling was a constant source of tension and conflict, and was diagnosed as schizophrenic in late adolescence. The youngest sibling frequently complained of being left out, and angrily criticized her parents for depriving her of what she needed as a child. Mary, however, felt that her childhood had been reasonable, her parents had done the best they could; she was the uncomplaining 'good' child. Anthony, for his part, grew up in a family where his father – a successful public figure – was frequently but erratically angry and contemptuous of him. He learnt to be constantly on watch for an attack, but also knew that there was no reliable guide as to when one would come. His mother had, during his childhood and adolescence, retreated into a quiet, withdrawn alcoholism.

In the early stages of therapy, it gradually emerged that Anthony and Mary each created for the other a repeat of their painful and unresolved difficulties from childhood. Anthony projected on to Mary his sense of his inadequacy: he 'knew' that she would find him wanting in the relationship. He found Mary's angry outbursts frightening, and more and more he resorted to his known strategy of trying to intuitively sense when she was upset and to accommodate to keep the peace. Thus, as when he was a child, he learnt never to initiate telling Mary what *he* thought, felt or wanted, but rather he waited for a cue from her, and then adapted his experience to her mood. Mary, for her part, initially thought she had found in Anthony's quiet and considerate presence a maturity she longed for in a partner – but he also turned out to be a man who seemed unable to be strong for her, however hard she tried to provoke or shame him into taking a stand. She increasingly experienced his concern to accommodate and keep the peace as intensely frustrating, just like her parents' failure to set clear boundaries with her disturbed and demanding younger sibling. She thus faced a choice in her relationship with him: to be self-contained and look after her own emotional needs, something she was expert at doing; or she could try to get Anthony to be there for her, strong and reliable, a response she had never been able to get from her well-meaning but ineffectual father. And so she was angry with Anthony – expressing some of the rage she had often felt, but denied, towards her father.

Or consider this relationship, where projection seems to have played a major role in the selection of a partner:

> The product of a home with an abusive and alcoholic father, and later with a chronically conflicted mother and step-father, Rupert presented as a young man who was impeccably groomed, very religious, deeply committed and conscientious in his professional role as a teacher. Always calm, he planned for everything, and intended to have a quiet, modestly successful, and ordered life. Even when talking about deeply distressing events in his adult life, he seemed neither to experience or show any emotion, talking about what had happened in a calm, rather flat and reasonable way.
>
> Rupert married a woman who was constantly demanding and complaining, and who, following a frightening and life-threatening health crisis, was now depressed, despairing and intensely angry. They had separated some eighteen months before seeking couples therapy. Neither wanted the marriage to end, not least because of their strongly held religious beliefs. Rupert genuinely believed that the problem was solely his wife's – that she was being self-indulgent and attention-seeking in being emotional and upset. Yet, he had in fact married someone who expressed in abundance the angry, chaotic and frightened parts of himself that he could never let himself be aware of or admit to.

Another way in which the agenda for relationship of each partner is important is that it is the basis for the 'invisible marriage' that is a part of every couple relationship:

> In relationship, each partner's unconscious fears and yearnings encounter the other's. Despite our conscious intentions, these unconscious fears and yearnings control our experience of the relationship. They are like the stagehands in a theatre production. They set up the props and backdrops that form the backdrop to our relationship, they play the background music that heightens our emotions, and at key times they hit a particular speech or action with a powerful spotlight that sets it apart from the rest of the action. While what we see is what happens 'onstage'

between ourselves and our partners, our unconscious fears and yearnings are busy controlling the meanings we attach to those actions. The term 'invisible marriage' refers to the unconscious factors that control how we feel and act in relationships.

(Shaddock 1998: 16)

The 'invisible marriage' is a way of describing the web of transferences operating between the partners. Writing about group therapy with couples, James Framo describes the way in which, even to group members who know nothing of psychodynamic theory, the transferential elements of a couple's relationship gradually come into focus:

> when members of the couples group give feedback to the couple in these early phases, they usually not only stick closely to reality factors, but also make fairly low-level observations: 'I think you're a very nice couple' or 'Maybe if you talked to your wife more, she might not crowd you so much'. When group members get to know each other as the weeks go by, however, the feedback becomes more sophisticated. The transference manifestations, as the partners interact, gradually become more apparent to the other group members. The group quickly picks up on such obvious behaviour as transference rages that are out of all proportion to the stimulus, or the way some people pursue so relentlessly a partner who clearly has nothing but contempt for them. Then these lay persons may give feedback of the order of: 'I don't know where it's coming from, but it seems to me your wife doesn't deserve the punishment you're dishing out to her', . . . or 'Boy, you sure expect a lot from a husband'.
>
> (Framo 1992: 20)

In a similar manner, in couples or family therapy, the invisible marriage – or, where family therapy is concerned, the invisible family – only starts to become apparent as the therapist comes to know the couple in more depth, and as he starts to become aware of the 'unspoken conversation' in the relationship.

The phenomenon of projective identification has been referred to in earlier chapters. This process, which involves a partner or child (or a therapist) coming to experience and express for a person some aspect of their own personality that the person cannot accept in themselves, is of particular importance in an understanding of the dynamics of couple and family relationships (Catherall 1992). Often, in couple relationships, the process is a mutual one.

Jack and Sue presented as a couple with an intolerable relationship. She expressed vitriolic anger at the slightest provocation, and he would then withdraw – emotionally, and often physically. There had been numerous separations in the course of their marriage of some twenty-four years, but they always seemed to end up back together again. Now, however, their children had left home, and Sue had a professional position that gave her both financial security and an increasing desire for a more intimate relationship; they were unsure whether they would survive as a couple.

Jack had experienced an extremely deprived childhood following the death of his mother when he was quite young. Brought up by his father as an only child – his older siblings either went to live with relatives or had left home – he moved from town to town in the Australian outback, involving frequent changes of school. He was often left alone while his father spent long periods in the pub. Now, as an adult, he presented as a tall, quiet, stoic man. He never expressed anger, either about his early experiences in life or about his present situation; nor did he talk about the pain of his childhood experiences. He worked in a tough occupation, where he was in all likelihood the butt of a great deal of anger and abuse, but talked about this in an unemotional, matter-of-fact way. In his marriage he saw himself as the powerless victim of Sue's rages: he couldn't tell her how he felt, but could only hide until the storm had passed, and then carry on as if nothing had happened. Sue, too, had experienced abuse and emotional trauma as a child, principally at the hands of her father. She found it very difficult to own or talk about her childhood pain, or the vulnerability she often experienced now as an adult. She yearned for an intimate relationship, where the vulnerable part of her could be cared for, but to even think about admitting to her vulnerability felt terrifying.

As therapy progressed, it became increasingly clear that both Jack and Sue projected the unacceptable and unowned parts of themselves into the other. Jack projected his anger into Sue, who then acted it out for him; he in turn could then criticize her anger as being unreasonable and punish her for it. Sue, for her part, projected her vulnerability into Jack: when he 'behaved like a wimp' and withdrew as a powerless, miserable little boy in the face of her anger, she in turn could attack the vulnerability in him. Gradually, both were able to start to own the unowned parts of themselves: Jack to experience his anger and Sue her neediness. As they did so, the destructive pattern of their relationship, which had held sway for so long, began to change; each began to allow the other to know about and respond to their emotional needs in a different way.

Seen in this way, projective identification allows the 'bad' or feared, unowned aspect of self to be expressed in a 'safe' way, and often in a way in which it can be more safely criticized or attacked. This has given rise to one of the 'practice wisdom' adages of relationship therapy: when a person persistently complains about or attacks a significant other, it is often useful to explore how the attribute that is complained about is experienced and owned (or disowned) by the person doing the complaining. Thus Sue's complaint about Jack's passivity and weakness might make us wonder about the vulnerable, passive part of her; and Jack's calm, rather helpless, complaint about Sue's anger might make us wonder about his anger.

Projective identification, which is an object relations theory concept, originates in the mother–baby relationship, and is observed not only between adult partners but also between parents and children (Box *et al.* 1981; J.S. Scharff 1989). But the experience of self that is split off and projected is not always a 'bad' or feared part of self; it may be a good or valued part of self, which is projected into the other for safe-keeping and then enjoyed in them.

## The process of conjoint therapy

One helpful way of thinking about how transference occurs and can be used therapeutically in couples or family therapy is provided by David and Jill Scharff (1991), who distinguish between contextual transference and focused transference. The Scharffs begin with the contrast between the mother providing the context for the relationship with the baby – making sure the baby is cared for, clean, warm, comfortable – and the mother's focused engagement with the baby in eye contact and attunement to the baby's experience. The former they call the 'arms-around holding' relationship; the latter they call 'centred holding'. From this they move to describe two forms of transference. First, the patient relates to the therapist in terms of their previous experience of 'arms-around holding' in relationships; these hopes and/or fears about being 'held' contribute to what they term the 'contextual' transference to the therapeutic situation. Second, the patient brings into the relationship with the therapist expectations and fantasies based upon specific experiences in focused engagement in earlier relationships; the hopes, fears, excitement and rejection involved in such experiences give rise to what the Scharffs term the 'focused' transference to the therapist.

In individual work, the contextual transference is in the foreground and must be addressed in the early phases of treatment. In couples or family therapy, while both types of transference are present, the Scharffs argue that they are experienced differently. In couples therapy, the partners bring to the therapy their developed focused transferences to each other; they also bring a shared contextual transference 'built around their shared hopes and fears about the therapist's capacity to provide therapeutic holding by shoring up their deficient ability to provide holding for themselves' (Scharff and Scharff 1991: 66). While individual partners or family members may develop focused transferences to the therapist, the focus needs to be on the therapist's experience of the couple or family *as* a couple or family, rather than as two individuals. This 'countertransference' – the therapist's own transference to the couple or family – thus becomes an important source of information for the therapist. To quote the Scharffs, referring here specifically to couples therapy:

> Experience with the couple resonates with the therapist's life experience of couples, especially those couples who have been or are primary in earlier and current life, including parents, prior relationships with partners in adolescence and adulthood, former marriages, previous therapeutic relationships, and current relationships with spouses or loved persons.
>
> We each have many versions of couples inside us, just as we have many versions of families inside. These versions express angry couples, loving couples, and idealised and feared couples. At different points in the transference, different aspects of the internal couple constellation and the corresponding affects will be sensed by therapists in the countertransference. The most immediate clue to the kind of relationship being stirred up inside is the set of emotions that come into play. This clue leads to the couple's contextual transference to the therapist and its resonance with their shared projective identifications or transferences to each other.
>
> (Scharff and Scharff 1991: 73)

Listening to the internal couple in the countertransference requires the therapist to have a capacity for 'negative capability' – in the poet Keat's phrase, the capacity to be in 'uncertainty and doubt without any irritable reaching out after fact and reason' (Scharff and Scharff 1991: 82).

Central to the process of couples and family therapy is the creation of a 'safe space' or a 'holding environment', where feelings, fears and thoughts, which cannot usually be voiced or responded to, can become available for reflection and response. In essence, this is where the transferences operating between the partners or between parents and children can be recognized and explored. in David Scharff's words:

> tolerance, taking in, reflecting, and digesting. These absorptive activities give us space to think and to analyse our own responses and countertransference. We model for the family this process of creating space for review . . . This is our contribution to creating mental and emotional space in which many things happen and can be spoken and felt, but especially in which projections can be re-examined.
>
> (D.E. Scharff 1989: 429)

Therapy with Rosemary and Gary provides some illustration of these processes.

Rosemary and Gary sought therapy some four years ago when they were on the point of separating. Both were professional people. They had two young children and they did not want to part, but Rosemary felt estranged from Gary and saw no future in the relationship. The therapist saw them for about ten sessions as a couple. The story that emerged was that Rosemary had, some four years previously, been diagnosed with a serious form of cancer and had every reason to expect that her condition could be terminal. She had survived, but in doing so had needed to undergo lengthy treatment that was in many ways quite dehumanizing; nobody had thought to discuss with her the emotional impact of the technology or to 'debrief' her. To avoid further emotional hurt, she did what she was prone to do – became emotionally self-sufficient and detached. Gary felt scared and powerless; and he did what he also tended to do – withdrew, became practical, and hoped 'it' would go away.

In the early therapy sessions, the therapist's countertransference to them as a couple was centred on the enormous emotional vulnerability and neediness in their relationship; conjoint couples therapy, with the likelihood of emotional engagement with each other, felt too frightening – in countertransference for the therapist, but in reality for them. Things improved marginally and they started to talk on a superficial level with each other; they decided that they could stay together, but with no great desire on Rosemary's part for any intimacy, and not much hope on Gary's part. Even to hold hands when out for a walk was too threatening for Rosemary.

It seemed that conjoint sessions would be too difficult for Rosemary, and so the therapist negotiated with them both that Rosemary would be seen on her own for a while. Individual therapy with Rosemary for about a year followed, during which she was able to work through much of the trauma of her illness and the treatment, and also came to recognize the template through which she had always viewed relationships – a template that saw intimacy as making herself unnecessarily vulnerable. In the individual therapy, the focus was initially on the contextual transference, involving the fear Rosemary had of becoming dependent on the therapist. Then the focus moved to aspects of her transference to the therapist that recreated aspects of her relationship with her father, from whom she needed to keep any vulnerability safely hidden. During this time there were occasional conjoint sessions to keep Gary informed of progress and to review how things were going for them as a couple.

When Rosemary felt she had gone as far as she wanted to with the individual therapy, the therapist had a number of sessions with Gary, focused on helping him to recognize his pattern of accommodating to Rosemary and avoiding anger or emotional intensity.

After a break of a few months, Rosemary and Gary felt ready to return to conjoint therapy. The contextual transference came into the foreground again, but the therapist's experience of being with them now was quite different. While they still had no sexual contact, and any physical contact was very cautious and limited – as Rosemary put it, she always made sure that the kitchen table was between them if they were alone together! – there was now a sense of subdued excitement in the room, which on occasions had a sexual edge to it. This was a couple who could now admit that they cared deeply for each other, and who both wanted but feared re-establishing sexual contact. The conjoint therapy now focused on a gradual opening up of the transferences operating between them that kept them so locked into a safe but unrewarding caution in their emotional and sexual relationship. They each began to talk with each other about experiences in their relationship, and in their earlier lives, which had not been shared before – initially by writing letters that they gave to each other in the session and talked about, but then increasingly by creating their own space for intimacy at home.

Working with Rosemary and Gary, it was the contextual transference that led – in this instance via a rather circuitous route – to the creation of a safe space for them, a space within which they could start to understand something of their transferences towards each other, and experiment with letting themselves experience each other differently.

Whatever format the therapy takes with couples – conjoint, concurrent or a mixture of the two modalities (Crawley and Grant 2001) – powerful existing transferences are usually brought into the therapy. The task of the therapist is to bring into the awareness of the couple these templates that so powerfully shape the pattern of the marital interaction, so that their impact can be opened for exploration by the couple. Understanding and respecting the reality and power of the 'invisible marriage' for the couple, together with some understanding of how it is impacting upon their therapist through the counter-transference, is in many ways a basic survival skill for the couples therapist.

## A resource for facilitating change in relationships

The intriguing and inevitable question in family and couples therapy is how deeply entrenched patterns of relating can change. Many models of family and couples therapy have developed over the years, each usually prescribing particular interventions that the therapist can make to facilitate change and, usually, a rationale for why the interventions are appropriate and likely to be successful. From a psychodynamic perspective, interventions that are effective in bringing about changes in relationships usually appear to have brought about – intentionally or otherwise – a shift in some aspect of the 'invisible marriage' or 'invisible family', the matrix of transferences and projections operating in the relationship system. This statement is not intended to be condescending or dismissive of models that do not espouse a psychodynamic orientation, but rather to open up another window through which the process of change can be understood, explored and consolidated.

Consider the following vignettes from different approaches to family or couples therapy:

A therapist working in the experiential tradition of Virginia Satir uses the technique of family sculpture to help members of a family become more aware of their feelings about each other. She enables the mother to talk about her real feelings about her first husband, who left when she was pregnant with her first child; he drank heavily, had several affairs during the three years that they were together, and has made no effort to stay in contact with his son. She goes on to talk about her fear that her son will become the sort of man his father was. At age 14 her son has been in increasing trouble at school for unruly behaviour and recently came home drunk after a party. Surprisingly, she has never made this connection before. Instead of being anxious and judgemental towards the son, the family now start to talk in an open and vulnerable way about their mutual hurt. It is the tentative beginning of what proves eventually to be a new pattern of relating between them, and indeed between the son and his step-father and step-siblings. There has been a shift in the invisible family; the mother's transference towards her eldest son no longer leads her to behave towards him in a way that leaves him feeling unloved and different to his step-siblings, and other transferences start to be modified as a consequence.

A therapist working in a structural family therapy framework sets a homework task that involves an estranged father and adolescent daughter spending regular time together. The intervention is a success. Over the next few weeks, they become increasingly relaxed with each other; he no longer sees her as 'totally selfish and spoilt', and she starts to enjoy a more friendly and teasing relationship with him. When they get angry with each other and fight, it no longer has the same feeling of despair and desperation about it, and their conflict no longer drives a wedge between husband and wife. In structural terms, there has been a strengthening of the parenting subsystem of the family, and a more flexible boundary established between father and daughter. From a psychodynamic perspective, the father no longer needs to project onto his daughter the feeling of being unloveable and misunderstood that was his experience in his own unhappy adolescence, and his daughter thus no longer needs to act out a role that invites him to repeat the critical and rejecting behaviour of his own father.

A couple who have a highly reactive and recriminatory relationship start to meet regularly with a therapist whose work is influenced by a constructivist approach. The therapist remains curious about their experience of each other, and they are encouraged to explore their story with her in a way that opens up new dimensions to the way they make sense of each other's behaviour. They go on to review the story each brought into their relationship about couples, relationships and marriage, and how that has shaped the meanings they each gave to their experiences of each other. After a few sessions, they are no longer so instantly reactive to each other, but are starting to engage in a more collaborative way – with the therapist, but also with each other. They begin to hear and understand each other in a different way – a different story or narrative unfolds – and this opens up new ways of responding apart from attacking and criticizing each other. From a psychodynamic perspective, there again has been a shift in the invisible marriage. They have begun to relate in a way that each experiences as empathic rather than wounding; their capacity to provide selfobject experiences for each other has increased.

A useful distinction is sometimes made between first-order change and second-order change (Watzlawick *et al.* 1974). 'First-order change' refers to a change in behaviour that is often a response to the therapy situation, but is not based on any underlying change in the pattern or dynamics of relationships between the partners or within the family. For example, after a few sessions a couple might report a decrease in the frequency of conflict between them, or the behaviour of a child who is an 'identified patient' in the family might appear to improve. Such change often does not last, however, once the therapy ends. By contrast, 'second-order change' is said to have occurred when there is a significant shift in the underlying patterning of relationships – the relationship system – that results in the problem or symptomatic behaviour becoming redundant. Second-order change in relationships involves a change in the way the parties to the relationship feel about and respond to each other *that emerges from a change in the sense of self of one or both partners*. In turn, this different way of responding to each other leads to further change and consolidation in their sense of self. For example, it is usual in couples therapy that each partner will enter therapy believing, at some level, that if their partner would change in some way, then their problems would be lessened or resolved. Initial attempts at change are likely to be based on bargaining or accommodating to the other – 'if I do X, you will have to do Y' – and this usually only leads to first-order change. Second-order change is more likely to begin when each partner reaches a point of wanting to behave or respond differently in the relationship *for themselves*. This inevitably involves taking more responsibility for their own experience and behaviour in some way and focusing on this, not on changing their partner.

We have suggested above that many of the interventions of family and couples therapy have the effect of modifying some aspect of the matrix of transferences and projections in the invisible marriage or family (Crawley and Grant 2001). Since transference and projection are unconscious processes, however, it will sometimes be helpful for the therapist to put forward a suggestion – in psychoanalytic language, 'make an interpretation' – about what might be happening in the relationship based on her or his understanding of the patterns of the invisible marriage or family. In doing this, the therapist is usually bringing into conscious awareness some aspect of one person's subjective or internal experience of the other and the way that this, in turn, has influenced the other partner's subjective experience in the relationship. For example:

> Sandra and George had a history of violence in their relationship, but they had survived this and reached a point where there seemed to be no likelihood of further violence. They still struggled with intimacy, however, with Sandra being constantly anxious and fearing that the marriage would – against all the evidence of their deep affection for each other – end in separation. On one occasion, Sandra described her sense of paralysing fear during a disagreement with George.

The obvious explanation was that this was a result of her memories of violent behaviour by him many years ago, but this didn't seem to ring true to her. As she discussed some of her other experiences of fear, she talked about the way in which her mother used to 'look right through me' when angry and not speak to her for hours or even days. The therapist suggested that when her husband became angry he became for that moment her mother, and she became terrified of the loss of her relationship with him, of being 'wiped out' by his rage. This led to an exploration of different sorts of anger – and the recognition that her husband's anger on this occasion was an expression of hurt and need, not a reaction of annihilating rage such as she had experienced with her mother. Her recognition of this made it possible for her to begin to respond differently to George when he was angry because he was hurt, which in turn led to George starting to express his needs more appropriately to her.

David and Joy's relationship was characterized by an underlying tension that was at odds with the depth of caring they felt for each other.

David was a successful professional, a powerful man who at first rather intimidated the therapist. It emerged that he was the middle of seven siblings in an intact but chaotic family. He learnt to survive by being intellectually smart and combative. Joy managed in the relationship by being accommodating to his rather brusque manner, but was becoming less willing to do so; hence the increased tension. They knew the facts of each other's backgrounds, but little of the lived emotional experience, despite a marriage of twenty-two years. Joy was often resentful of David's refusal to hear any hint of criticism of his siblings, several of whom she found rather disorganized and insensitive.

Joy responded positively to a homework task of spending an evening finding out more about each other's childhood experiences, but David wouldn't reciprocate and talk about his childhood. Discussing this in the next session, he explained that he thought Joy would mock him and not understand, and he would be very hurt as a result – an unexpected response from such an articulate and self-assured man. Exploring this, David talked of his mother's lack of emotional attunement or sensitivity, his father's preoccupation with work, and the highly competitive relationship between the siblings – an emotionally barren childhood. To express need or vulnerability was indeed to invite ridicule, disappointment and hurt; yet his siblings had been all he had and he was loath to speak critically of them. The therapist suggested that the same template was operating in his marriage – to express vulnerability would be to open himself to disappointment or hurt, even though he loved Joy deeply and yearned for more intimacy. Their relationship soon began to change; he came to see Joy's complaints about their relationship as an expression of her wanting closeness rather than as an attack and, consequently, began to take the risk of being more open and vulnerable with her.

## Conclusion

This chapter has described some of the ways in which an under-standing of transference and projection can be of use to the coun-sellor or psychotherapist working with couples and families. As in other modalities of therapy, transference and projection provide one way of understanding some of the complexities of the therapeutic relationship, and suggest possibilities for intervention. Additionally and uniquely, transference and projection also provide a valuable means for understanding some of the complexities of the entity being worked with, the relationships between partners and between parents and children, since transference is an inevitable component of these relationships.

# C H A P T E R  **8**

# Recognizing and responding
# to transference

## Introduction

As will be clear from the earlier chapters, the concepts of transference and projection are complex. Transference in particular has acquired a range of meanings within the field of psychoanalysis, where it originated. In this chapter, we address the practical question of how an understanding of these concepts can be put to use by the therapist.

First, however, a word of caution. Working with the transference – that is, seeking to foster the development of transference and then understanding and interpreting it – is the core of the therapeutic method used in psychoanalysis, as well as a central element in psychodynamic psychotherapy. To use transference in this specific way requires training and detailed clinical supervision. If possible, therapists seeking to use the transference in their work should gain the experience of receiving their own personal psychotherapy which focuses on the use of the transference. If this is not possible, then at the very least they should seek regular supervision from a therapist who is experienced in this way of working.

However, as we have sought to show in earlier chapters, transference does not only appear in the work of psychodynamically trained practitioners. Transference is an ubiquitous phenomenon that is present in all relationships, especially therapeutic relationships, whether it is recognized or not. Therefore, in seeking to set out some guidelines for the use of transference, our focus is the therapist who does not have specific training in psychoanalytic or psychodynamic therapy, but who acknowledges the validity of the concept of transference and who wishes to begin to recognize and respond to this phenomenon in their clinical work.

## The essential features of transference

The guidelines which follow are a response to three questions about transference that are frequently asked:

- How can the therapist recognize the presence of transference in the therapeutic relationship?
- How does responding to transference assist with the process of therapy and with facilitating change for the client?
- When and how should the therapist respond to transference?

To respond to these questions, we inevitably draw upon psychodynamic theory, since it is this tradition that has been most concerned to recognize and understand transference. As we have shown in earlier chapters, however, therapists working in other approaches to counselling and psychotherapy still encounter the phenomenon of transference. The ideas that we set out here in response to these three basic questions are intended to enable the reader, whatever approach to therapy they adopt, to become more aware of transference issues in their own clinical work.

Various definitions and understandings of transference have been discussed in earlier chapters. Before starting to try to answer our questions, it may be valuable to identify three of the essential features of transference that we have discussed in this book.

*Transference as an unconscious organizing activity*

New experiences must be integrated into the person's existing knowledge of the world: this process of organizing new experience, which is constantly engaged in at an unconscious level, becomes partially visible in the transference element of relationships. This process is ubiquitous in that it occurs in all relationships, but it has particular meaning in the special situation of the therapeutic relationship, where it can be viewed as a mirror to the client's internal self.

Many different writers, approaching transference in different ways, use surprisingly similar metaphors for describing the way in which transference enables the person to assimilate and respond to new experiences. Freud talked of 'templates', while psychotherapists developing short-term models of therapy have described the 'core conflictual relationship theme' (Luborsky and Crits-Christoph 1998; Book 1998), the 'core relationship problem' (Horner 1998) or the 'cyclical maladaptive pattern' (Levenson 1995), all phrases that reflect the source of transference. Psychotherapists working in the inter-subjective framework speak of 'thematic structures' of the individual's personal subjective world; cognitive-behavioural therapists increas-ingly refer to 'cognitive schemas'; and existential therapists refer to the client's 'self-and-world construct system'. All these terms appear to be describing a significant relationship theme or pattern in the person's life that he or she uses to organize and make sense of experiences with others, and which will inevitably be re-enacted in various ways in therapy and in the relationship between the client and the therapist. In the words of Stolorow *et al.* (1987: 37), 'Trans-ference is conceived . . . as the expression of a universal psycholo-gical striving to organise experience and construct meanings'.

### The complex origins of transference

This process of organizing experience is shaped by past learning in significant relationships in the early years of life. It reflects un-resolved issues and painful experiences from childhood, as well as reflecting the ways the person has had positive experiences which provide a greater sense of fulfilment in their life.

Children manage relationships – especially with the key figures in their lives, such as parents – the best way that they can. When rela-tionships are difficult or traumatic, the child's primary concern is survival and achieving some degree of security. From these childhood experiences, patterns develop that are carried over into adult life and relationships, including the relationship with a therapist. These patterns mean that the client reads the therapist's behaviour in particular ways that make sense to them in the light of earlier experi-ences, and responds to the therapist in ways that are congruent with their earlier organization of experience. Sometimes such patterns are not appropriate in adult life and thus often work against relation-ships being effective. Yet when viewed from the perspective of the person's subjective view of their world when they were a child, and thus viewed as transference, the patterns start to make sense.

Occasionally transference *is* straightforward and obvious; the therapist is experienced exactly as a key figure, usually parental, from childhood. More often, the transference will involve the gradual exploration and disentanglement of less obvious links. The therapist may, for example, represent a parent who was needed but not available at important times to provide the understanding or nurturing that was longed for but never received. Or the way the therapist is experienced may involve elements of more than one significant relationship, with the therapist being viewed simultaneously in both a positive and a feared way. The possibilities are endless, which means – as we discuss below – that any understanding of the transference elements of the client–therapist relationship should always be held tentatively, as a hypothesis to be confirmed or disconfirmed, rather than as an unassailable fact.

### Transference involves persistent perceptions of the other

There is a quality of persistence to the perceptions involved in transference, a persistence that resists the evidence that otherwise might reasonably be expected to modify the client's perceptions of the therapist.

As postmodernism is making increasingly clear, perception is always subjective and in that sense contains elements of distortion. What is different about the distortion involved in the transference aspects of a relationship, whether between marital partners or between client and therapist, and what distinguishes it from the real relationship, is the persistence with which the distorted view is held. A husband sees his wife as 'meddling' in his business affairs while he was away on an overseas trip, rather than as having tried to assist him; nothing will persuade him even to consider any other way of viewing her behaviour. A client tells a therapist he is untrustworthy because he is a male and she cannot possibly confide in him, despite several months of therapy where the 'therapeutic frame' of time, boundaries, empathy and respect has been meticulously maintained. However, although these patterns reflect the inner world of the client, the therapist also contributes to the pattern of transference that evolves in a particular therapeutic relationship.

Although transference is usually seen to involve an element of distortion, it is also always connected in some way, however approximately, to the therapist's responses and reactions to the client. This suggests that transference cannot be seen simply as a 'quality' within the client, which can be observed independently of the therapist's presence and behaviour. This, in turn, challenges the traditional assumption that the therapist needs to be 'neutral', in the sense of being unresponsive to the client, so as not to 'contaminate' the transference; such neutrality is itself a behaviour by the therapist, which the client will unconsciously seek to assimilate into his or her understanding of the therapeutic situation. The notion of distortion is often questioned today because of its implication that there is a 'real reality' that only the therapist knows about. Gill (1982) suggests replacing the idea of distortion with the notion of situations as being open to multiple interpretations, including events in the therapeutic relationship; each interpretation needs to be explored afresh by therapist and client.

Against this backdrop we can now address the three questions about transference that are the focus of this chapter.

## Recognizing transference

One way of identifying transference is phenomenologically, focusing on the actual behaviour and experience of the client and therapist in the therapeutic relationship. We begin by briefly reviewing from this perspective three dimensions of transference that are frequently referred to in the literature: positive and negative transferences, the erotic transference and the selfobject transferences.

### Positive and negative transferences

A distinction is commonly made between *positive* and *negative* transferences. A positive transference is said to be one in which positive feelings towards the therapist are experienced by the client – feelings of warmth, love, admiration, trust, affection, and so on. By contrast, a negative transference is said to involve feelings of anger, fear, resentment, contempt or mistrust towards the therapist. Therefore, one of the key questions for the therapist, which always needs to be held in the therapist's mind, is about the affective tone of the way the client appears to relate to him.

A positive transference is a necessary condition for therapeutic change, according to psychodynamic psychotherapists. In brief psychodynamic psychotherapy, the early development of a positive transference is usually seen as a necessary indication that brief therapy is appropriate, while the failure to establish a positive transference early in the therapy is usually taken as an indication that longer-term work will be necessary. Likewise, in the cognitive therapies, there is a focus on the 'collaborative relationship' that is so essential between therapist and client for interventions to be effective, while humanistic-existential therapies stress the need for 'unconditional positive regard' so that a positive relationship can be activated between therapist and client. Basch (1995: 29) puts it as follows:

> The capacity to rely on the therapist's guidance and the support that the therapeutic process *per se* offers are essential for any and all psychotherapeutic work. The presence of the positive transference indicates that the therapist is being equated unconsciously with the loving and helpful parent the patient had or longed for, and once this transference has been made, the therapist's words carry all the authority, influence, and power of such a parent. Under the influence of the positive transference, a patient's sense of isolation, loneliness, and helplessness is sufficiently ameliorated to lower anxiety and permit the appropriate interventions of the therapist to have an effect. By the same token, until a meaningful connection can be made between patient and therapist, the latter's interventions – no matter how correct in principle – will fail to be effective.

While a positive transference is a necessary background condition for therapy, a negative transference, like the erotic transference discussed shortly, always needs to be explored: otherwise it has the potential to derail the therapy.

Michael was an intelligent, good-looking man in a professional occupation. He attended couples therapy with his wife Monica. While Monica was emotionally very expressive, Michael was the calm, reasonable partner in the relationship, rarely showing or admitting to any strong feelings and remaining rather distant and aloof from the therapist and from the process of the early sessions.

In the third session, the therapist began by asking whether a simple diary-keeping homework task suggested in the previous session had been useful. Michael responded that he had not done it, and went on to explain that it didn't seem to him to make much sense. He expressed this in a quiet and reasonable way; but as the therapist listened, he sensed in himself considerable anger. Assuming that this was a countertransference to Michael, that he was perhaps experiencing an emotion that Michael did not feel safe to express, he said something to Michael along the lines of 'I hear what you are saying; but I also get the sense that, although you are not showing it, you are perhaps quite angry. Do you think that's possible?' Michael responded that he was indeed feeling very angry – not so much about the exercise, more about the fact that he was having to talk to a stranger about personal things and how anxious that made him feel. Asked if he had any ideas as to why he should find it so anxiety-provoking to talk about personal things, he went on to talk about his relationship with his mother, whom he described as very 'cutting' and sarcastic – 'She would interrupt you before you had said two words' – and who often left him feeling shamed and inadequate. This, in turn, led to a useful discussion of aspects of the dynamics of Monica's and Michael's relationship; by the end of the session Michael seemed to be relating to the therapist with a sense of hope and trust about the process of therapy. A negative transference to the therapeutic context and to the therapist had begun to change to a positive one.

We should also note that sometimes what could be described as a positive transference in other circumstances can become negative and disabling – for example, where positive regard for the therapist turns into idealization. Similarly, what is often seen as negative, the expression of anger, may be a positive step when it is expressed by the normally passive client, even if the anger is still to some extent transferred rather than wholly deserved by the therapist.

*Erotic transference*

Another aspect of transference, and one that can be disconcerting for therapists until they recognize it as a transference phenomenon, is the erotic transference. As the term implies, this involves the client developing a positive transference that is characterized by sexual or erotic feelings for the therapist. Therapy is a relationship characterized by the self-disclosure of very personal experiences by the client and by an empathic and interested response from the therapist. It is thus an intimate relationship, and it is hardly surprising that the feelings that are sometimes transferred to the therapist are of an erotic or sexual nature. Sometimes the client will give a direct or indirect indication that this is the nature of their feelings for the therapist. At other times the therapist must be aware of other cues – for example, perhaps a change in the way the client dresses or presents themselves – and, if it seems appropriate, gently explore these.

> Wendy had been in weekly, then fortnightly, therapy for about eight months following the ending of her marriage. She had started to make good progress, coming to understand her chronically poor self-esteem that had its origin in her relationship with her depressed mother and self-effacing father. Then, after a break of several weeks over the summer holidays, she reported that she felt as if the therapy had stalled and nothing much seemed to be happening for her in the sessions. Discussion of this did not reveal any apparent reason connected with the holiday break.
>
> Wendy came to the next session saying that she wanted to talk about a disturbing dream. In the dream, she had been kissing her 10-year-old son when the kiss suddenly became unmistakably erotic and sexual. She awoke at that point and had felt very uncomfortable for the following couple of days leading up to the session. She had no idea what the dream meant; she certainly was not aware of any inappropriate sexual feelings for her son.
>
> Assuming that this might be an aspect of transference, the therapist referred to the sense she had reported in the previous session of the therapy having 'stalled', and asked if she had been aware of any change in her feelings about him recently. After a few moments of silence, Wendy hesitantly said that she supposed she had to admit that she had been aware of having sexual fantasies about the therapist for the past few weeks. This led to an initially awkward, but ultimately very productive, exploration of her experience of herself as a sexual person. Issues to do with sexuality had been discussed before in the therapy, but in a more detached way; now there was an immediacy that was new. As issues about the avoidance of anything to do with sexuality in her childhood and her yearning for recognition from her father were worked through, Wendy began for the first time to accept and enjoy an awareness of her sexuality.

An erotic transference, like a negative transference, has the potential to derail the therapy, as well as the potential to lead into an exploration of important aspects of the client's experience. If the erotic transference is not addressed and explored, important issues may be ignored, or the client may leave therapy prematurely. If an erotic transference is not recognized and respected as a transference phenomenon, there is also the danger of the therapist acting out his or her countertransference experience and the possibility of a sexually exploitative relationship developing between therapist and client. If this leads to physical sexual acting out, it is virtually always damaging to the client, which is why all professional codes of ethics prohibit such activity. It is important to recognize, however, that a seductive or sexualized pattern of interaction in the therapeutic relationship is also potentially very damaging for a client.

One of the aspects of therapy that can make it easier to deal with an erotic transference productively is the existence of a clear 'therapeutic frame'. The therapeutic frame consists of the arrangements and protocols that surround and contain the therapy – issues such as clarity and punctuality about the timing and length of sessions, rules about physical contact between client and therapist (especially in therapies where physical touch is a component of the therapeutic process), and the management of contact outside of sessions. The clearer and more 'solid' the therapeutic frame is, the safer the therapy time and space will become for the client, and the easier it will be to contain and explore a wide variety of experiences, including sexual and erotic feelings.

### Selfobject transferences: mirroring, idealizing and twinship transferences

In Chapter 4, a description was given of the particular contribution made to the understanding of transference by Heinz Kohut and the self psychology tradition that evolved from his work. Kohut identified the 'selfobject transferences' – patterns of relating that are evoked in the therapeutic relationship as a consequence of the client's particular areas of deficit in earlier development. Wolf provides a helpful way to understand the difficult notion of 'selfobject':

> The most fundamental finding of self psychology is that the emergence of the self requires more than the inborn tendency to organise experience. Also required are the presence of others, technically designated as *objects*, who provide certain types of experiences that will *evoke* the emergence and maintenance of

the self. The perhaps awkward term for these is *selfobject experiences*, usually abbreviated to *selfobjects*. Proper selfobject experiences favour the structural *cohesion* and energetic *vigour* of the self; *faulty* selfobject experiences facilitate the *fragmentation* and *emptiness* of the self. Along with food and oxygen, every human being requires age-appropriate selfobject experiences from infancy to the end of life.

(Wolf 1988: 11, emphasis in original)

In the empathic, non-judgemental milieu of the therapeutic relationship, selfobject needs that were not met at earlier stages of life are reactivated and lead to a pattern of relating to the therapist – selfobject transferences – that allows a resumption of the development of a cohesive self. The most frequently referred to selfobject transferences are the mirroring transference and the idealizing transference.

In the mirroring transference, the need of the client for recognition, admiration and praise reflects an early developmental need for acceptance and confirmation of the self by the selfobject. Kohut referred to 'the gleam in the mother's eye, which mirrors the child's exhibitionistic display, . . . confirm(ing) the child's self esteem and, by gradually increasing selectivity of these responses, begins to channel it into realistic directions' (Kohut 1971: 116). Mirroring by the therapist is a way of relating in the therapeutic relationship, not a technique; it needs to be appropriate to the developmental need of the client – as baby, as pre-schooler, as adolescent. For example, a client was describing his delight in trying out and exploring new experiences as a consequence of starting to have a beginning sense of himself as a separate person. The therapist's response was along these lines: 'What comes to mind as you tell me that is the joy a toddler has as he finds all sorts of new things and puts them in his mouth, discovering those that feel and taste good and those that don't'.

In the idealizing transference, the client's need is for 'an experience of merging with a calm, strong, wise, and good selfobject', which gives rise to the 'more or less disguised admiration of the analyst, his or her character and values, or by defences against this transference, such as prolonged and bitter depreciation of the analyst' (Wolf 1988: 126). Basch (1988: 141) describes this as 'the need to be united with someone one looks up to, and who can lend one the inspiration, the strength, and whatever else it takes to maintain the stability of the self system when one is endangered, frustrated, or in search of meaning'.

With the selfobject transferences, the question that the therapist must hold in mind is not so much about the affective tone of the way the client relates to him, but what the client seems to want from him – to be admiring and responsive, or to be an admired and perhaps somewhat idealized figure to be identified with.

## The two triangles of transference

A helpful way of starting to understand transference in the therapeutic relationship has been provided by Malan (1979) with his concept of 'the two triangles': the *triangle of conflict* and the *triangle of the person*. Malan himself was bringing together ideas from earlier writers in putting forward this way of understanding the dynamics of the therapeutic situation (Menninger 1958). Later writers, especially in the developing field of brief psychodynamic psychotherapy, have drawn upon and extended this idea (Vaillant 1997; Fosha 2000). The usefulness of the idea of the two triangles lies in the fact that, 'between them they can be used to represent almost every intervention that a therapist makes; and that much of a therapist's skill consists in knowing which parts of which triangle to include at any given moment' (Malan 1979: 80).

The triangle of conflict focuses on intrapsychic conflict. The client experiences a feeling or an impulse; this feeling or impulse may well give rise to anxiety, in which case the client will defend or protect themself against the anxiety. These three elements – feeling or impulse, anxiety, and defence – give us the three elements of this first triangle.

The process of defence may take a variety of forms. For example, the result may be that the person is not aware of an anxiety-arousing feeling because they have denied it or repressed it. Alternatively, the defence used may disguise the nature of an anxiety-arousing feeling, as in the defence of reaction formation: the angry feeling becomes solicitousness for the other, or sexual interest or curiosity becomes disapproval of anything sexual. Or the defence may seek to bring the feeling under control, as in the process of intellectualization. The original feeling or impulse is outside the client's awareness; all that is visible to the therapist is the behaviour that results from the defensive strategy, and perhaps some residue of the anxiety that is generated by the feeling or impulse. This first triangle is depicted in Figure 8.1.

The second triangle, the triangle of the person, concerns the focus of both the initial anxiety-arousing feeling and of the defensive

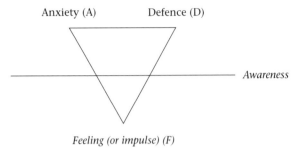

Anxiety (A)     Defence (D)

Awareness

*Feeling (or impulse) (F)*

**Figure 8.1** The triangle of conflict (adapted from Malan 1979).

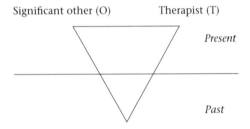

Significant other (O)     Therapist (T)

*Present*

*Past*

Significant figure from past (parent) (P)

**Figure 8.2** The triangle of the person (adapted from Malan 1979).

solution. There are three possible figures at a point in time who could be the focus for the client (see Figure 8.2): the therapist (T), another person (O) in the client's current environment, or a significant figure from the past (P).

When the experience of a feeling or impulse gives rise to anxiety, the origin of this anxiety is usually with some significant figure in the person's past, often a parent. This link has, however, been forgotten or, more accurately, repressed, and is outside the client's awareness. Thus the focus of the anxiety and/or defensive behaviour is often on a current figure, either the therapist or, less directly, a significant other in the client's environment. Literally, the experience generated by the feeling – that is, the anxiety – is transferred to another figure. Much of the work of therapy involves seeking to understand the feeling or impulse behind the defence in the triangle of conflict, and the original figure with whom the anxiety was generated by this feeling in the triangle of the person – that is, seeking to understand the elements of each triangle and the relationship between them.

Two examples, one from longer therapy and one from short-term work, help make this clearer.

Simon grew up in a chaotic family. His mother had been severely abused and traumatized as a victim of the holocaust, spending part of her adolescence in a concentration camp. She was later diagnosed as having a 'severe borderline personality disorder'; from Simon's account, she was chaotic, manipulative, and had several lengthy spells in a psychiatric hospital. His father, also a survivor of a war-time trauma in his childhood and adolescence, appeared to cope well with life: he was a 'man of the world', always smartly dressed and appearing confident. Yet, as Simon described him, it appeared that he was highly narcissistic, unable to empathize with or appreciate anyone's needs except his own. Simon's parents had separated when he was about 8 years old; he lived with his mother (or was in an institution when she was hospitalized), but spent time with his father whenever he could. He described cycling long distances to visit his father, hoping that his father would be home and that they could spend time together.

Simon presented for therapy as a very depressed man. He initially described his childhood as having been ordinary and happy – a defence against the intolerable emotional pain he had often felt. For the first two years of therapy, he was frequently suicidal. Gradually, a strong therapeutic alliance formed and it became clear that the therapist had become an extremely important figure in his life. One of the features of the therapeutic relationship was that Simon clearly idealized the therapist, and never acknowledged any anger – indeed, never any frustration or irritation – with the therapist. This was so even in the face of some of the usual disruptions that occur in therapy and which can reasonably be expected to generate some disappointment or anger on the part of the client. Simon denied ever feeling angry with anyone and was surprised that people sometimes saw him as angry, yet it gradually became clear that, in some circumstances and with some people, Simon was able to be aware of feeling irritated or angry; this was especially the case with some of his former work colleagues who had, in his opinion, treated him very unfairly.

Eventually, a point was reached where it was possible for Simon to begin to reflect upon his experience of the therapy more directly and to begin to explore his feelings about the therapist. The picture that emerged was that:

- as the therapist became more significant to Simon – 'I think I wouldn't have survived if it hadn't been for you' – it aroused considerable anxiety for him if he had any angry or critical thoughts towards the therapist: he feared he might lose him, as he had feared losing the other 'life-line' in his life, his father;
- he often felt very hurt and angry with his father for not being available and responsive to him or recognizing how important he was in Simon's life – 'a life-line'; he was terrified as a child that if he expressed any anger or criticism towards his father, he would lose him, 'the only bit of warmth in my life';
- the defensive strategy that he used with the therapist, turning any angry feeling or impulse into an overly solicitous manner and idealizing the therapist, was the same strategy that he had learnt as a means of protecting himself from experiencing or expressing the dangerous angry feelings he had for his father at times as a small boy;
- as Simon was able to explore his occasional angry feelings towards the therapist, so he was able to start to face his highly ambivalent feelings towards his father; this, in turn, became the first step in building a stronger sense of 'self', with an appropriate sense of entitlement, and the beginning of a different pattern of relating in important personal relationships.

In the triangle of conflict, the feeling (F) of anger (or the impulse to attack and punish) aroused anxiety (A) that he would lose the therapist's regard and be rejected. His defence (D) against this was to transform his anger into being rather ingratiating and eager to please the therapist; for a long time, this was all the therapist saw of Simon's experience. In the triangle of the person, the origin of the anxiety about anger was with his father (P), but this was transferred to the therapist (T), to whom Simon related in the same (defensive) way that he had related to his father. Gradually, Simon was able to let the therapist know that he could be angry, but he did so not by owning his anger with his father or, less directly, with the therapist, but by talking about his anger with his former work colleagues (O). As therapy progressed, he could let himself experience the original feeling of anger without having to defend against it, and experience it with the person with whom it originated, his father. The sequence of exploration went from his eagerness to please to the feeling of anger, from the anger with his work colleagues (transference), to his anger with the therapist (transference), to his original anger with his father.

Peter was referred for therapy relating to his controlling and at times rather aggressive behaviour in his workplace. A contract of ten sessions was negotiated with his employer under an Employee Assistance Programme. In the first session, Peter was extremely aggressive with the therapist. He arrived late for the session and answered questions the therapist put to him in a contemptuous, monosyllabic manner. When asked what he thought about coming to see the therapist, he stated that the therapy was a waste of time; he knew all about counselling, he could tell what the therapist was going to ask before he asked it, everything was so predictable: but he had to come or he would suffer in his career. The therapist – who was aware of his own increasing anger as the session went on, a not unreasonable countertransference! – ended the session by indicating why he thought therapy might be worthwhile for Peter, but also pointing out that Peter's angry and uncooperative attitude was not likely to contribute to a good outcome. He stated that Peter had some choices about how he used the sessions, but he was willing to spend the time with him whatever he decided.

In the second session, Peter was more cooperative, and it was possible to find out a bit about his earlier life experience. Peter had been in the middle of a large family of twelve siblings. It was an intact family and the parents cared for the children. However, money was scarce, as were time and attention. Peter had experienced several painful things during his childhood, including witnessing the death in an accident of an older sibling to whom he was close. He didn't recall anyone being aware of his unhappiness and he learnt to cope with his own emotional state without turning to or relying on anyone else. To show vulnerability was an invitation to be ridiculed or shamed.

The picture emerged of Peter as a sensitive man beneath a rather rough exterior. Originally a tradesman – and by all accounts a very skilled one – he had later gained some academic qualifications and now found himself in a career where he needed to have well-developed interpersonal skills. He talked about how he was good when dealing with practical issues in his work, but when faced with emotional issues to which there was no apparent practical solution, he felt powerless and useless. In coming to see the therapist he had experienced himself coming into a situation where he expected to be found wanting – that is, having to talk about emotions; he expected to be shown up as vulnerable and inadequate, and consequently to feel shamed. By the third session, the anger with the therapist (a strong negative transference) had gone. In its place was a positive transference, with the therapist experienced as an idealized other with whom he could identify and learn. Therapy became a positive experience for both Peter and the therapist.

In the triangle of conflict, Peter experienced a feeling (F) of vulnerability, which led to anxiety; he defended (D) against this by behaving 'tough', behaving in an angry and contemptuous manner that was the opposite of what he really felt. In the triangle of the person, the anger was directed towards the therapist (T) in the transference, but the real source of the anxiety about vulnerability lay in his experiences of unrecognized vulnerability as a child (P). In previous situations in his work where Peter had felt vulnerable and inadequate, he had been angry and controlling with colleagues (O), the source of the referral to therapy. Had the therapist not recognized the initial anger as transference, he might well have decided that pursuing therapy with Peter was inappropriate in light of his hostility and apparent unwillingness to participate.

## Transference and change

If therapists are to make constructive use of the transference, they need to have their own understanding or rationale – their own sketch map – of how focusing on the transference can be a source of change for the client. Such a picture is built up over the course of a therapist's career, continually being refined in the reflexive process between, on the one hand, reading and understanding of theory and, on the other hand, increased clinical experience. Here we briefly outline two motifs about change that run through the psychodynamic literature where transference is a central feature of the therapeutic process. Other traditions have their own and somewhat similar motifs – for example, the psychological schema in cognitive-behavioural therapy, or the 'here-and-now experience' of experiential approaches to therapy.

The first motif is captured by the phrase 'making the unconscious conscious', a phrase that is frequently used to describe the essential core of the therapeutic process as seen from the perspective of psychoanalysis or psychodynamic psychotherapy. What this means, specifically, depends upon the theoretical orientation of the therapist. Indeed, each theoretical position has its own understanding of what is involved in 'making the unconscious conscious', and often it is a matter of the relative emphasis placed upon the curative factors, rather than of absolute distinctions.

For some therapists from a more classical psychoanalytical orientation, 'making the unconscious conscious' means discovering, through the exploration and interpretation of the transference, traumatic or unresolved issues from childhood that result in emotional or psychological difficulty in later life; and then enabling the client to gain insight into the effects of these experiences on their current life. The emphasis here is on the client gaining insight into the working of their own individual unconscious mind, especially into the sources of anxiety for them and the defensive strategies that they adopt to manage their anxiety.

Other therapists, from the relational and intersubjective traditions within psychodynamic therapy, see the process of 'making the unconscious conscious' not so much as gaining insight into repressed trauma and its consequences, but rather as bringing into consciousness the way that the client constructs meaning out of their experience. Thus the client learns to recognize (and will be able to begin to modify) the template through which they sift and assimilate all experiences; this template is seen most clearly in the transference that develops between client and therapist. This may often, of course, involve acquiring an understanding of aspects of their early life (including perhaps the lack of certain experiences) that led to the development of the template in its unique form for them; but the essence of change is seen as lying more in understanding how the here-and-now experience with the therapist is constructed. Thus, for example, Stolorow and his colleagues state: ' ... "making the unconscious conscious" refers to the interpretive illumination of the patient's unconscious organising activity, especially as this becomes manifest within the intersubjective dialogue between patient and analyst' (Stolorow *et al.* 1988: 12).

The second motif is the importance that is attached to the client's experience of the relationship with the therapist. Some therapists view the therapeutic relationship as a vehicle for the gaining of insight by the client. Here the therapeutic relationship becomes the *means* by which insight is acquired, but has no intrinsic importance in itself. The emphasis is, indeed, upon 'analysis', an essentially intellectual activity. For other therapists, particularly again from the relational approaches to psychodynamic theory (as well as in the humanistic tradition, even if they do not always use the term 'transference'), the therapeutic relationship becomes the source of a 'corrective emotional experience'. That is, the relationship with the therapist becomes *itself* the main source of change for the client, as old traumatic experiences are re-enacted in the therapeutic relationship, but are responded to differently. Out of this new relational experience comes growth and change – and, perhaps as a bonus, insight.

One example of an approach to change that focuses on the relational experience of the client in the therapeutic relationship is provided by Shane *et al.* (1997) in their recent book *Intimate Attachments: Towards a New Self Psychology*. The authors observe that the term 'transference' has come to be used so widely that it is often a source of conceptual confusion rather than of clarity. They adopt a position that transference is a relational configuration within therapy, 'wherein the past does more than infuse the present . . . it seems to overwhelm it. Transference in our model . . . describes a relational configuration wherein there is a predominance of old patterning over new, that is, of assimilation over accommodation' (p. 71).

From this, they go on to suggest that three relational configurations can be identified during the analytic or therapeutic process, only the first of which is correctly seen as a transference relationship:

- The 'old self with old other' relational configuration. This is described as a current relationship with the analyst wherein both the analyst and the self are perceived by the patient . . . as figures predominantly organised on the basis of traumatic relational experiences with significant, traumatogenic others from the past' (p. 103). Trauma is conceived as including experiences of loss, intrusion, deprivation and neglect as well as threats or perceived threats to physical well-being.

- The 'old self with new other' relational configuration. This is described as a transitional state, where the old self of the client 'feel(s) caught in old, traumatised ways, incapable of feeling differently about himself or herself, but nevertheless is beginning to experience the analyst as a person different from past, traumatising others, a novel other, one without prototype in the patient's life' (p. 104).

- The 'new self with new other' relational configuration. This third configuration represents 'a developing capacity for organising current experiences of self with other in new and different ways instead of persistently organising self and self with other based on ... traumatogenic experience from the past' (pp. 104–5).

## Responding to transference and projection

How, then, should the therapist go about starting to explore transferential and projective aspects of the therapeutic relationship with their clients?

The starting point is that the therapist will always need to be *listening* in a particular way to the client. Listening to the content and the affective quality of what the client is saying, but *also* listening for hints, buried in what is being communicated, about the particular transference or projection that might be present in the way in which the client is relating to the therapist at this point in time. The hints are sometimes obvious, but are usually more subtle. This is where the 'two triangles' referred to earlier provide a useful framework for starting to tease out and develop hypotheses about the less obvious aspects of the therapeutic relationship.

This leads to an important point: we must always remember that, in dealing with transference and projection, we are in the realm of subjective experience, of the unconscious, of the symbolic, and of the 'as if'. This can raise a dilemma for the therapist. The client is often initially unsure about or resistant to understanding their experience or behaviour in transferential or projective terms; the therapist needs to be sufficiently confident in presenting this as a possibility that it is likely to be considered by the client. Yet, on the other hand, the therapist must avoid the trap of being dogmatic, of being 'the one who knows the truth' about the client's experience. The word 'interpretation' sometimes can appear to assume a rather magical or mysterious quality for some therapists; the very word 'interpretation' can at times sound rather authoritarian. It is perhaps helpful to think of 'making an interpretation' as simply 'putting a different possibility' to the client – an *alternative* interpretation of behaviour or experience, not necessarily a *correct* interpretation. An interpretation of the transference should be an 'invitation' to explore another way of looking at experience; for example, 'You are telling me how angry you are about your friend letting you down; I wonder, is it possible you are also letting me know that you are angry with me for being sick and missing the last two sessions we had scheduled?' This is far less dogmatic than: 'Your anger is really with me for missing the last two sessions, not with your friend who let you down'.

Part of the solution to this dilemma is for the therapist to develop their own way of explaining, in the early stages of therapy, why exploring the relationship between therapist and client is an important component of the therapeutic process. This may be an initial explanation that is part of the process of establishing the therapeutic frame, but it usually needs to be made concrete and immediate when the therapist starts to explore and interpret a possible transference aspect of the relationship.

> In the first meeting with Bill, it was agreed that he would meet with the therapist regularly for a period of time to seek an understanding of a dilemma he was in about an extramarital affair. He was concerned about hurting his wife and letting his children down if he left the marriage. The therapist said something like the following: 'One of the things we will do is to explore the way you experience your relationship with me as it develops over the coming weeks. We need to do that because many of the ways in which you instinctively relate to people will be repeated in our relationship, and it will be a useful source of understanding for us if we can explore our relationship in a way that often can't happen in other relationships'.
>
> In the next session, Bill talked at great length and with some obvious anxiety about having ended his relationship with his lover: but he did so in a controlled, rational way, trying to explain his reasons and reactions. The therapist eventually commented: 'I sense that you are telling me about an experience that must have been very painful, deciding not to see Jill again when she has been so very important to you.

I imagine that you must be experiencing some very strong feelings about this. But I also experience you trying to explain to me what has happened in a very rational and responsible way, and not really letting me see the strength of your feelings. Perhaps this is an example of where we need to start to explore our relationship. I wonder if I'm right about how you are managing your feelings as you talk to me this evening; and if so, where you learned to do that?' Rather a wordy intervention perhaps – but Bill slowed down, began to talk in a much more congruent way about the loneliness of a childhood where he had always had to accommodate to his anxious mother, and spoke of the shame he had felt whenever he let her down. All of this was rich material for going on to explore his dilemma about staying in an emotionally rather barren marriage, or leaving to be with a woman he loved passionately.

An important lesson from the self psychology tradition is that the empathic stance of the therapist is of central importance when exploring the transference. Kohut (1984) makes this point in a thought-provoking way. He begins by describing a case presentation where the therapist told a client at the end of a session that a forthcoming session would need to be cancelled because the therapist would be away. In the next session, the client was silent and withdrawn, and the therapist eventually made an interpretation about this, using Kleinian language – along the lines that the client's basic perception of the therapist had shifted, she had become the bad, cold, non-feeding breast instead of the good, warm, feeding breast; that the client experienced sadistic rage against her, wanting to 'tear into her' by using biting language, but defended herself against these impulses by becoming silent and withdrawn. Kohut comments that, to his surprise, this 'far-fetched interpretation' elicited a very favourable response from the client. How was this to be explained? Was it that the content of the interpretation was correct? Kohut explains the outcome in the following way:

> could it be that, even though the content of the interpretation was wrong, the interpretation itself was still right? I think so. To my mind the interpretation was right in its essential message to the patient. Its specific content was of negligible importance and should be understood as being the non-specific carrier of the essential meaning that was transmitted.

And what was this meaning? . . . as far as the patient was concerned the analyst had said no more than this: you are deeply
upset about the fact that one of your appointments was cancelled. It is this simple but, I believe, profound human message,
expressed with human warmth, that the patient heard – never
mind the transference revival of the archaic experience of the
bad breast.

(Kohut 1984: 94)

He continues:

What is the nature of the therapeutic effect of psychoanalytic
therapy on the analysand? Does the foregoing vignette bring us
closer to an answer to this crucial question? I believe that it
does if we keep in mind the self psychological principle that
therapeutic interventions consist of two separate, identifiable,
but interdependent steps, . . . which, together, constitute the
substance of the basic therapeutic act . . . understanding and
explaining.

(Kohut 1984: 94)

In other words, the intervention was helpful to the client because
the interpretation was experienced as coming out of an 'experience
near' stance by the therapist, an empathic understanding of the
client's experience. Getting our understanding of the transference or
a projection correct in theoretical terms is perhaps less important
than the manner in which we use our awareness of the transference
to explore the client's experience. What matters is what the client
experiences in the relationship with the therapist as the transference
is explored: does the client feel that their subjective experience is
*understood* before an explanation is given for it? Needless to say, not
everyone would agree with Kohut's position, but it provides a
good principle to guide the therapist who is starting to explore the
transference with their clients.

## Conclusion

In this final chapter, we have highlighted several principles that
are important in responding to transference and to projections of a
similar kind, principles that have been discussed in more detail in
the earlier chapters of the book. We have set out some practical

guidelines for therapists who wish to use an understanding of these concepts in their work.

As we have sought to show, the phenomenon that Freud first observed and labelled 'transference' is ubiquitous in human relationships. Transference is not restricted to relationships between client and therapist. Nor does transference cease to exist or to be less important simply because the therapist works within a model or framework that does not use the term 'transference', or because he or she does not regard the phenomenon – whatever descriptive term is used to describe it – as important. It follows that an awareness of the nature of transference phenomena is important for all therapists, regardless of theoretical orientation. From this awareness needs to come an understanding of ways of responding to transference which are congruent with the model of therapy being used. In this volume, we may have concentrated upon the psychodynamic understanding of transference – the 'home base' as it were of transference – but we have observed the links to this concept in other major therapeutic modalities. Transference and projection are indeed 'mirrors to the self', mirrors that can reflect the richness of the inner world and illuminate the patterns of interaction with others. Responded to and understood well, these concepts, translated into practice, enable clients to have more opportunities to make the kinds of relationships they want, both with others and with themselves.

# References

Agin, S. and Fodor, I.E. (1996) The use of the core conflictual relationship theme method in describing and comparing gestalt and rational emotive behavior therapy with adolescents, *Journal of Rational-Emotive and Cognitive-Behavior Therapy*, 4: 173–86.

Andersen, S.M. (1995) Meaning ascription in the elicitation of emotional response: automatic and non-conscious processing, *Psychological Inquiry*, 6: 197–204.

Andersen, S.M. and Berk, M.S. (1998) Transference in everyday experience: implications of experimental research for relevant clinical phenomena, *Review of General Psychology*, 2: 81–120.

Anderson, E.M. and Lambert, M.J. (1995) Short-term dynamically-oriented psychotherapy: a review and meta-analysis, *Clinical Psychology Review*, 15: 503–14.

Appignanesi, L. and Forrester, J. (2000) *Freud's Women*. London: Penguin.

Baker, H.S. and Baker, M.N. (1987) Heinz Kohut's self psychology: an overview, *American Journal of Psychiatry*, 144: 1–9.

Baker, S. (1997) Dancing the dance with dissociatives: some thoughts on countertransference, projective identification and enactments in the treatment of dissociative disorders, *Dissociation*, 10: 214–22.

Bartholomew, K., Henderson, A. and Dutton, D. (2001) Insecure attachment and abusive intimate relationships, in C. Clulow (ed.) *Adult Attachment and Couple Psychotherapy: The 'Secure Base' in Practice and Research*. London: Brunner-Routledge.

Basch, F. (1988) *Understanding Psychotherapy: The Science Behind the Art*. New York: Basic Books.

Basch, F. (1995) *Doing Brief Psychotherapy*. New York: Basic Books.

Bauer, G.P. and Mills, J.A. (1994) Patient and therapist resistance to use of the transference in the here and now, in G.P. Bauer (ed.) *Essential Papers on Transference Analysis*. Northvale, NJ: Jason Aronson.

Beck, A.T. (1991) Cognitive therapy: a 30-year retrospective, *American Psychologist*, 46: 368–75.

Beck, A.T. and Weishaar, M. (1989) Cognitive therapy, in A. Freeman, K. Simon, L. Beutler and H. Arkowitz (eds) *Comprehensive Handbook of Cognitive Therapy*. New York: Plenum Press.

Beck, A.T., Freeman, A. and Associates (1990) *Cognitive Therapy of Personality Disorders*. New York: Guilford Press.

Beck, J.S. (1995) *Cognitive Therapy: Basics and Beyond*. New York: Guilford Press.

Bion, W.R. (1962) *Learning from Experience*. London: Heinemann.

Bollas, C. (1987) *The Shadow of the Object: Psychoanalysis of the Unthought Known*. London: Free Association Press.

Book, H. (1998) *How to Practice Brief Psychodynamic Psychotherapy: The CCRT Method*. Washington, DC: American Psychological Association.

Bowlby, J. (1969) *Attachment and Loss: Vol. 1. Attachment*. New York: Basic Books.

Bowlby, J. (1988) *A Secure Base: Clinical Applications of Attachment Theory*. London: Routledge.

Box, S., Copley, B., Magagna, J. and Moustaki, E. (eds) (1981) *Psychotherapy with Families: An Analytic Approach*. London: Routledge.

Bretherton, I. (1991) The roots and growing points of attachment theory, in C.M. Parkes, J. Stevenson-Hinde and P. Marris (eds) *Attachment Across the Life Cycle*. London: Routledge.

Brewin, C.R. (1997) Psychological defences and the distortion of meaning, in M. Power and C.R. Brewin (eds) *The Transformation of Meaning in Psychological Therapies*. New York: Wiley.

Bugental, J.F.T. (1965) *The Search of Authenticity: An Existential-Analytic Approach to Psychotherapy*. New York: Holt, Rinehart & Winston.

Bugental, J.F.T. and McBeath, B. (1995) Depth existential therapy: evolution since World War II, in B. Bongar and L.E. Beutler (eds) *Comprehensive Textbook of Psychotherapy: Theory and Practice*. Oxford: Oxford University Press.

Catherall, D. (1992) Working with projective identification in couples, *Family Process*, 41(4): 355–68.

Celani, D.P. (1993) *The Treatment of the Borderline Patient: Applying Fairbairn's Object Relations Theory in the Clinical Setting*. Madison, CT: International Universities Press.

Clark, A.J. (1995) Projective identification in counselling: theoretical and therapeutic considerations, *Canadian Journal of Counselling*, 29: 37–49.

Clark, A.J. (1998) *Defense Mechanisms in the Counselling Process*. Thousand Oaks, CA: Sage.

Clark, D.A. (1995) Perceived limitations of standard cognitive therapy: a consideration of efforts to revise Beck's theory and therapy. *Journal of Cognitive Psychotherapy: An International Quarterly*, 9: 153–72.

Clark, R.W. (1980) *Freud: The Man and the Cause*. New York: Random House.

Clarkson, P. (1999) *Gestalt Counselling in Action*. London: Sage.

Clayton, L. (1982) The use of the cultural atom to record personality change in individual psychotherapy, *Journal of Group Psychotherapy, Psychodrama and Sociometry*, 12: 112–17.

Clulow, C. (ed.) (2001) *Adult Attachment and Couple Psychotherapy: The 'Secure Base' in Practice and Research*. London: Brunner-Routledge.

Clulow, C. and Mattinson, J. (1989) *Marriage Inside Out: Understanding Problems of Intimacy*. London: Penguin.

Cohn, H.W. (1989) Man as process: existential aspects of psychotherapy, in F. Flach (ed.) *Psychotherapy*. New York: Norton.

Crawley, J. and Grant, J. (2001) The self in the couple relationship – part 2, *Psychodynamic Counselling*, 7: 461–74.

Crits-Christoph, P. (1992) The efficacy of brief dynamic psychotherapy: a meta-analysis, *American Journal of Psychiatry*, 149: 151–8.

Crits-Christoph, P. (1998) The interpersonal interior of psychotherapy, *Psychotherapy Research*, 8: 1–16.

Dallos, R. and Draper, R. (2000) *An Introduction to Family Therapy: Systemic Theory and Practice*. Buckingham: Open University Press.

Davanloo, H. (ed.) (1978) *Basic Principles and Technique in Short-Term Psychotherapy*. New York: Spectrum.

Dicks, H. (1967) *Marital Tensions*. London: Tavistock.

Dobson, K.S. and Shaw, B.F. (1995) Cognitive psychotherapies in practice, in B. Bongar and L.E. Beutler (eds) *Comprehensive Textbook of Psychotherapy*. Oxford: Oxford University Press.

Donner, S. (1993) The treatment process, in H. Jackson (ed.) *Using Self Psychology in Psychotherapy*. Northvale, NJ: Jason Aronson.

Dorpat, T.L. and Miller, M.L. (1992) *Clinical Interaction and the Analysis of Meaning: A New Psychoanalytic Theory*. Hillsdale, NJ: The Analytic Press.

Ehrenberg, D.B. (1992) *The Intimate Edge: Extending the Reach of Psychoanalytic Interaction*. New York: Norton.

Elliott, R. and Greenberg, L.S. (1995) Experiential therapy in practice: the process-experiential approach, in B. Bongar and L.E. Beutler (eds) *Comprehensive Textbook of Psychotherapy: Theory and Practice*. Oxford: Oxford University Press.

Ellis, A. (1994) *Reason and Emotion in Psychotherapy: A Comprehensive Method of Treating Human Disturbances*. Secaucus, NJ: Birch Lane.

Fairbairn, W.R.D. (1954) *An Object Relations Theory of the Personality*. New York: Basic Books.

Fenichel, O. (1945) *The Psychoanalytic Theory of Neurosis*. New York: Norton.

Fiske, S. (1982) Schema-triggered affect: application to social perception, in M.S. Clarke and S.T. Fiske (eds) *Affect and Cognition: The 17 Annual Carnegie Symposium on Cognition*. Hillsdale, NJ: Erlbaum.

Flaskas, C. and Perlesz, A. (1996) *The Therapeutic Relationship in Systemic Therapy*. London: Karnac Books.

Foreman, S.A. (1996) The significance of turning passive into active in control mastery theory, *Journal of Psychotherapy Practice and Research*, 5: 106–21.

Fosha, D. (2000) *The Transforming Power of Affect: A Model for Accelerated Change*. New York: Basic Books.

Foulkes, S.H. (1975) *Group-Analytic Psychotherapy: Methods and Principles*. London: Gordon & Breach.

Fox, J. (ed.) (1987) *The Essential Moreno: Writings on Psychodrama Group Method and Spontaneity by J.L. Moreno MD*. New York: Springer.

Framo, J. (1992) *Family-of-Origin Therapy: An Intergenerational Approach*. New York: Brunner/Mazel.

Frankl, V. (1969) *Will to Meaning*. New York: World Publishing.

Freud, S. ([1911] 1958) Psycho-analytic notes upon an autobiographical account of a case of paranoia (Dementia Paranoias), in J. Strachey (ed.) *The Standard Edition of the Complete Psychological Works of Sigmund Freud*, Vol. 12. London: Hogarth.

Freud, S. ([1912] 1958) The dynamics of transference, in J. Strachey (ed.) *The Standard Edition of the Complete Psychological Works of Sigmund Freud*, Vol. 12. London: Hogarth.

Freud, S. and Breuer, J. ([1895] 1955) Studies on hysteria, in J. Strachey (ed.) *The Standard Edition of the Complete Psychological Works of Sigmund Freud*, Vol. 2. London: Hogarth.

Gackenbach, J. (ed.) (1998) *Psychology and the Internet*. San Diego, CA: Academic Press.

Gaston, L., Goldfried, M.R., Greenberg, L.S., Horvath, A.O., Raue, P.J. and Watson, J. (1995) The therapeutic alliance in psychodynamic, cognitive-behavioral, and experiential therapies, *Journal of Psychotherapy Integration*, 5: 1–26.

Gay, P. (1988) *Freud: A Life for Our Time*. London: Macmillan.

Gelso, C.J. and Hayes, J.A. (1998) *The Psychotherapy Relationship*. New York: Wiley.

Gendlin, E.T. (1968) The experiential response, in E.F. Hammer (ed.) *Use of Interpretation in Therapy: Technique and Art*. New York: Grune & Stratton.

Gill, M.M. ([1979] 1990) The analysis of the transference, in R. Langs (ed.) *Classics in Psycho-analytic Technique*. Northvale, NJ: Jason Aronson.

Gill, M.M. (1982) *The Analysis of Transference*, Vol. 1. New York: International Universities Press.

Gill, M.M. (1994) *Psychoanalysis in Transition*. Hillsdale, NJ: The Analytic Press.

Glickauf-Hughes, C. (1997) Teaching students about primitive defenses in supervision, *The Clinical Supervisor*, 15: 105–13.

Glickauf-Hughes, C., Reviere, S.L., Clance, P.R. and Jones, R.A. (1996) The integration of object relations theory with gestalt techniques to promote structuralization of the self, *Journal of Psychotherapy Integration*, 6: 39–69.

Goldfried, M.R. (1995) *From Cognitive-Behavior Therapy to Psychotherapy Integration: An Evolving View*. New York: Springer.

Gomez, L. (1997) *An Introduction to Object Relations*. London: Free Association Books.

Grant, J. (1989) Lighting the inner light: understanding personal change in the training of personal counsellors, paper presented at the Australia-New Zealand Psychodrama Association Conference, Perth, WA, January.

Grant, J. (1997) When one model is not 'good enough' therapy: the use of psychodynamic psychotherapy with a panic disorder client, *Psychodynamic Counselling*, 3: 49–62.

Grant, J. (2000) Women managers and the gendered construction of personal relationships, *Journal of Family Issues*, 21: 963–85.

Grant, J. and Crawley, J. (2000) Demystifying transference: understanding and using transference in individual and couples therapy, paper presented at the Psychotherapy Australia Conference, Dallas Brooks Centre, Melbourne, VIC, July.

Grant, J. and Crawley, J. (2001) The self in the couple relationship – part 1, *Psychodynamic Counselling*, 7: 445–59.

Grant, J. and Porter, P. (1994) Women managers: the construction of gender in the workplace, *Australian and New Zealand Journal of Sociology*, 30: 149–64.

Greenberg, L.S., Lietaer, G. and Watson, J.C. (1998) Experiential therapy: identity and challenges, in L.S. Greenberg, J.C. Watson and G. Lietaer (eds) *Handbook of Experiential Psychotherapy*. New York: Guilford Press.

Greenson, R. (1967) *The Technique and Practice of Psychoanalysis*, Vol. 1. New York: International Universities Press.

Guidano, V.F. (1987) *Complexity of the Self*. New York: Guilford Press.

Guidano, V.F. (1988) A systems, process-oriented approach to cognitive therapy, in K.S. Dobson (ed.) *Handbook of Cognitive Behavioral Therapies*. New York: Guilford Press.

Guntrip, H. (1969) *Schizoid Phenomena, Object Relations, and the Self*. New York: International Universities Press.

Guntrip, H. (1971) *Psychoanalytic Theory, Therapy and the Self*. London: Karnac Books.

Gustafson, J.P. (1997) *The Complex Secret of Brief Psychotherapy*. Northvale, NJ: Jason Aronson.

Harman, B. (1996) Is there a future for the here and now?, *The Gestalt Journal*, 19: 101–8.

Heard, W.G. (1995) The unconscious functions of the I–it and I–thou realms, *The Humanistic Psychologist*, 23: 239–58.

Heller, N.R. and Northcut, T.B. (1999) Clinical assessment, in T.B. Northcut and N.R. Heller (eds) *Enhancing Psychodynamic Therapy with Cognitive Behavioral Techniques*. Northvale, NJ: Jason Aronson.

Hinshelwood, R.D. (1995) The social relocation of personal identity as shown by psychoanalytic observations of splitting, projection, and introjection, *Philosophy, Psychiatry and Psychology*, 2: 185–204.

Hinshelwood, R.D. (1999) Countertransference, *International Journal of Psycho-Analysis*, 80: 797–818.

Hirsch, I. (1998) The concept of enactment and theoretical convergence, *Psychoanalytic Quarterly*, 67: 78–101.

Holmes, J. (1998) The changing aims of psychoanalytic psychotherapy: an integrative perspective, *International Journal of Psychoanalysis*, 79: 227–40.

Holmes, P. (1991) Classical psychodrama, in P. Holmes and M. Karp (eds) *Psychodrama: Inspiration and Technique*. London: Tavistock/Routledge.

Holmes, P. (1992) *The Inner World Outside: Object Relations Theory and Psychodrama*. London: Tavistock/Routledge.

Horner, A.J. (1998) *Working with the Core Relationship Problem in Psychotherapy*. San Francisco, CA: Jossey-Bass.

Horowitz, M., Marmar, C.H., Krupnick, J., Wilner, N., Kaltreider, N. and Wallerstein, R. (1997) *Personality Styles and Brief Psychotherapy*. Northvale, NJ: Jason Aronson.

Hycner, R. and Jacobs, L. (1995) *The Healing Relationship in Gestalt Therapy*. New York: The Gestalt Journal Press.

Jacobs, M. (1998) *The Presenting Past*. Buckingham: Open University Press.

Jacobson, N.S. (1989) The therapist–client relationship in cognitive behavior therapy: implications for treating depression, *Journal of Cognitive Psychotherapy: An International Quarterly*, 3: 85–96.

Jones, E. (1964) *Sigmund Freud: Life and Work* (edited and abridged by L. Trilling and S. Marcus). Harmondsworth: Penguin.

Juni, S. (1997) Conceptualizing defense mechanism from drive theory and object relations perspectives, *American Journal of Psychoanalysis*, 57: 149–66.

Kahn, M. (1997) *Between Therapist and Client: The New Relationship*, revised edn. New York: W.H. Freeman.

Kellerman, P.F. (1985) Charismatic leadership in psychodrama, *Journal of Group Psychotherapy, Psychodrama and Sociometry*, 38: 84–95.

Kelly, G.A. (1955) *The Psychology of Personal Constructs*. New York: Norton.

Kernberg, O. (1987) Projection and projective identification: developmental and clinical aspects, *Journal of the American Psychoanalytic Association*, 35: 795–819.

Kernberg, O. (1997) The nature of interpretation: intersubjectivity and the third position, *Annual of Psychoanalysis*, 25: 97–110.

Kerr, M.E. and Bowen, M. (1988) *Family Evaluation: An Approach Based on Bowen Theory*. New York: Norton.

Klein, M. (1946) Notes on some schizoid mechanisms, *International Journal of Psycho-Analysis*, 27: 99–110.

Knapp, P. (1991) Self-other schemas: core organizers of human experience, in M.J. Horowitz (ed.) *Person Schemas and Maladaptive Interpersonal Behavioral Patterns*. Chicago: University of Chicago Press.

Kohlenberg, R.J. and Tsai, M. (1989) Functional analytic psychotherapy, in N.S. Jacobson (ed.) *Psychotherapists in Clinical Practice*. New York: Guilford Press.

Kolenberg, R.J. and Tsai, M. (1991) *Functional Analytic Psychotherapy*. New York: Plenum Press.

Kohut, H. (1971) *The Analysis of the Self*. New York: International Universities Press.

Kohut, H. (1977) *The Restoration of the Self*. New York: International Universities Press.

Kohut, H. (1984) *How Does Analysis Cure?* Chicago, IL: University of Chicago Press.

Kovel, J. (1992) Naming and conquest, *Monthly Review*, 44: 49–60.

Kyrios, M. (1998) A cognitive-behavioural approach to the understanding and management of obsessive-compulsive personality disorder, in C. Perris and P.D. McGorry (eds) *Cognitive Psychotherapy of Psychotic and Personality Disorders*. New York: Wiley.

Langs, R. (1992) *A Clinical Workbook for Psychotherapists*. London: Karnac Books.

Lantz, J. and Kondrat, M.E. (1996) Integration of problem-oriented and mystery-centered approaches in existential psychotherapy, *Journal of Contemporary Psychotherapy*, 26: 295–305.

Layden, M.A., Newman, C.G., Freeman, A. and Morse, S.B. (1993) *Cognitive Therapy of Borderline Personality Disorder*. Needham Heights: Allyn & Bacon.

Levenson, H. (1995) *Time-Limited Dynamic Psychotherapy*. New York: Basic Books.

Lichtenberg, P., van Beusekom, J. and Gibbons, D. (1997) *Encountering Bigotry: Befriending Projecting Persons in Everyday Life*. Northvale, NJ: Jason Aronson.

Likierman, M. (2001) *Melanie Klein: Her Work in Context*. London: Continuum.

Linehan, M. and Kehrer, C.A. (1993) Borderline personality disorder, in D.H. Barlow (ed.) *Clinical Handbook of Psychological Disorders*, 2nd edn. New York: Guilford Press.

Luborsky, L. and Crits-Christoph, C. (1998) *Understanding Transference*, 2nd edn. Washington, DC: American Psychological Association.

Lynch, V.L. (1993) Basic concepts, in H. Jackson (ed.) *Using Self Psychology in Psychotherapy*. Northvale, NJ: Jason Aronson.

Mahoney, M.J. (1991) *Human Change Processes*. New York: Basic Books.

Malan, D.H. (1963) *A Study of Brief Psychotherapy*. New York: Plenum Press.

Malan, D.H. (1979) *Individual Psychotherapy and the Science of Psychodynamics*. London: Butterworth.

Mallinckrodt, B., Gantt, D.L. and Coble, H.M. (1995) Attachment patterns in the psychotherapy relationship: development of the client attachment to therapist scale, *Journal of Counselling Psychology*, 42: 307–17.

Mann, J. (1973) *Time-Limited Psychotherapy*. Cambridge, MA: Harvard University Press.

Manzano, J., Palacio Espasa, F. and Zilkha, N. (1999) The narcissistic scenarios of parenthood, *International Journal of Psychoanalysis*, 80: 465–76.

Marcus, D.M. (1998) Self-disclosure: the wrong issue, *Psychoanalytic Inquiry*, 18: 566–79.

Maslow, A. (1968) *Toward a Psychology of Being*, 2nd edn. Princeton, NJ: Van Nostrand.

May, R. (1990) On the phenomenological bases of therapy, in K. Hoeller (ed.) *Readings in Existential Psychology and Psychiatry*. Seattle, WA: Review of Existential Psychology and Psychiatry.

Meichenbaum, D.H. (1995) Cognitive-behavioral therapy in historical perspective, in B. Bongar and L.E. Beutler (eds) *Comprehensive Textbook of Psychotherapy*. New York: Oxford University Press.

Menninger, K. (1958) *Theory of Psychoanalytic Technique*. New York: Basic Books.

Mitchell, S.A. (1991) Wishes, needs, and interpersonal negotiations, *Psychoanalytic Inquiry*, 11: 147–70.

Mitchell, S.A. (1999) Attachment theory and the psychoanalytic tradition: reflections on human relationality, *Psychoanalytic Dialogues*, 9: 85–107.

Moreno, J. (1946/1977) *Psychodrama*, Vol. 1. Beacon, NY: Beacon House.

Moreno, J. (1959) *Psychodrama*, Vol. 2. Beacon, NY: Beacon House.

Morgan, H. and Thomas, K. (1996) A psychodynamic perspective on group processes, in M. Wetherell (ed.) *Identities, Groups and Social Issues*. London: Sage.

Natterson, J.M. (1986) Interpretation: clinical application, in M. Nichols and T. Paolino, Jr. (eds) *Basic Techniques of Psychodynamic Psychotherapy*. Northvale, NJ: Jason Aronson.

Newton, P.M. (1995) *Freud: From Youthful Dream to Mid-Life Crisis*. New York: Guilford Press.

Nichols, M.P. (1987) *The Self in the System*. New York: Brunner/Mazel.

Nichols, M.P. and Schwartz, R.C. (2001) *Family Therapy: Concepts and Methods*, 5th edn. Boston, MA: Allyn & Bacon.

Northcut, T.B. (1999) Integrating psychodynamic and cognitive-behavioral therapy: a psychodynamic perspective, in T.B. Northcut and N.R. Heller (eds) *Enhancing Psychodynamic Therapy with Cognitive Behavioral Techniques*. Northvale, NJ: Jason Aronson.

Ogden, T.H. (1982) *Projective Identification and Psychotherapeutic Technique*. New York: Jason Aronson.

Ornstein, A. (1986) Supportive psychotherapy: a contemporary view, *Clinical Social Work*, 14: 14–30.

Ornstein, P.H. and Ornstein, A. (1985) Clinical understanding and explaining: the empathic vantage point, in A. Goldberg (ed.) *Progress in Self Psychology*, Vol. 1. New York: Guilford Press.

Padesky, C.A. (1996) Developing cognitive therapist competency: teaching and supervision models, in P. Salkovskis (ed.) *Frontiers of Cognitive Therapy*. New York: Guilford Press.

Perls, F.S. (1988) *Gestalt Therapy Verbatim*. New York: The Center for Gestalt Development.

Perls, F.S., Hefferline, R.G. and Goodman, P. (1969) *Gestalt Therapy: Excitement and Growth in the Human Personality*. New York: Julian Press.

Peyton, E. and Safran, J.D. (1998) Interpersonal process in the treatment of narcissistic personality disorders, in C. Perris and P.D. McGorry (eds) *Cognitive Psychotherapy of Psychotic and Personality Disorders*. New York: Wiley.

Pine, F. (1990) *Drive, Ego, Object, and Self: A Synthesis for Clinical Work*. New York: Basic Books.

Pine, F. (1998) *Diversity and Direction in Psychoanalytic Technique.* New Haven, CT: Yale University Press.

Potash, H.M. (1994) *Pragmatic-Existential Psychotherapy with Personality Disorders.* Madison, NJ: Gordon Handwerk.

Pretzer, J. (1998) Cognitive-behavioral approaches to the treatment of personality disorders, in C. Perris and P.D. McGorry (eds) *Cognitive Psychotherapy of Psychotic and Personality Disorders.* New York: Wiley.

Racker, H. (1957) The meanings and uses of countertransference, *Psychoanalytic Quarterly,* 26: 303–57.

Rafaelsen, L. (1996) Projections, where do they go?, *Group Analysis,* 29: 143–58.

Reid, E. (1998) The self and the internet: variations on the illusion of one self, in J. Gackenbach (ed.) *Psychology and the Internet.* San Diego, CA: Academic Press.

Rennie, D. (1998) *Person-Centred Counseling: An Experiential Approach.* New York: Sage.

Rhodes, R.H., Hill, C.E., Thompson, B.J. and Elliott, R. (1994) Client retrospective recall of resolved and unresolved misunderstanding events, *Journal of Counselling Psychology,* 31: 473–83.

Rosenfield, H. (1987) *Impasse and Interpretation.* London: Tavistock.

Rowan, J. (1983) *The Reality Game.* London: Routledge.

Rowan, J. (1992) Humanistic psychotherapy: what is humanistic psychotherapy?, *British Journal of Psychotherapy,* 9: 74–83.

Rudd, M.D. and Joiner, T. (1997) Countertransference and the therapeutic relationship: a cognitive perspective, *Journal of Cognitive Psychotherapy: An International Quarterly,* 11: 231–50.

St. Clair, M. (1986) *Object Relations and Self Psychology: An Introduction.* Monterey, CA: Brooks/Cole.

Safran, J.D. and Greenberg, L.S. (1986) Hot cognition and psychotherapy process: an information-processing/ecological approach, in P.C. Kendall (ed.) *Advances in Cognitive-Behavioural Research and Therapy,* Vol. 5. New York: Academic Press.

Safran, J.D. and Segal, Z.V. (1990) *Interpersonal Process in Cognitive Therapy.* New York: Basic Books.

Salzberger-Wittenberg, I. (1970) *Psychoanalytic Insight and Relationships: A Kleinian Approach.* London: Routledge.

Sanders, D. and Wills, F. (1999) The therapeutic relationship in cognitive therapy, in C. Feltham (ed.) *Understanding the Counselling Relationship.* London: Sage.

Sandler, J. (ed.) (1989) *Projection, Identification, Projective Identification.* London: Karnac Books.

Sandler, J. and Rosenblatt, B. (1962) The concept of the representational world, *Psychoanalytic Study of the Child,* 17: 128–45.

Sayers, J. (2000) *Kleinians: Psychoanalysis Inside Out.* London: Polity Press.

Schank, R.C. and Abelson, R.P. (1977) *Scripts, Plan, Goals, and Understanding.* Hillsdale, NJ: Erlbaum.

Scharff, D.E. (1989) Transference, countertransference, and technique in object relations family therapy, in J.S. Scharff (ed.) *Foundations of Object Relations Family Therapy*. Northvale, NJ: Jason Aronson.

Scharff, D.E. and Scharff, J.S. (1987) *Object Relations Family Therapy*. Northvale, NJ: Jason Aronson.

Scharff, D.E. and Scharff, J.S. (1991) *Object Relations Couple Therapy*. Northvale, NJ: Jason Aronson.

Scharff, J.S. (ed.) (1989) *Foundations of Object Relations Family Therapy*. Northvale, NJ: Jason Aronson.

Scharff, J.S. and Scharff, D.E. (1998) *Object Relations Individual Therapy*. Northvale, NJ: Jason Aronson.

Scharfman, M.A. (1992) The therapeutic relationship and the role of transference, in M.J. Aronson and M.A. Scharfman (eds) *Psychotherapy: The Analytic Approach*. Northvale, NJ: Jason Aronson.

Searles, H. (1965) *Collected Papers on Schizophrenia and Related Subjects*. New York: International Universities Press.

Segal, H. (1975) A psychological approach to the treatment of schizophrenia, in M. Lader (ed.) *Studies of Schizophrenia*. Ashford: Headley.

Shaddock, D. (1998) *From Impasse to Intimacy: How Understanding Unconscious Needs can Transform Relationships*. Northvale, NJ: Jason Aronson.

Shaddock, D. (2000) *Contexts and Connections: An Intersubjective Approach to Couples Therapy*. New York: Basic Books.

Shaffer, A. (1995) When the screen is not blank: transference to the psychodrama director in theory and clinical practice, *Journal of Group Psychotherapy, Psychodrama and Sociometry*, 48: 9–20.

Shane, M., Shane, E. and Gales, M. (1997) *Intimate Attachments: Towards a New Self Psychology*. New York: Guilford Press.

Shmueli, A. and Clulow, C. (1997) Marital therapy: definition and development, *Current Opinion in Psychiatry*, 10(3): 247–50.

Siegel, A. (1996) *Heinz Kohut and the Psychology of the Self*. London: Routledge.

Siegel, J. (1992) *Repairing Intimacy: An Object Relations Approach to Couples Therapy*. Northvale, NJ: Jason Aronson.

Sifneos, P.E. (1979) *Short-Term Dynamic Psychotherapy*. New York: Plenum Press.

Skynner, R. (1976) *Separate Persons. One Flesh: Principles of Marital and Family Psychotherapy*. London: Constable.

Skynner, J. and Cleese, J. (1984) *Families and How to Survive Them*. London: Methuen.

Slipp, S. (1981) *The Technique and Practice of Object Relations Family Therapy*. Northvale, NJ: Jason Aronson.

Slipp, S. (1984) *Object Relations: A Dynamic Bridge between Individual and Family Treatment*. New York: Jason Aronson.

Solomon, I. (1995) *A Primer of Kleinian Therapy*. Northvale, NJ: Jason Aronson.

Solomon, M. (1989) *Narcissism and Intimacy: Love and Marriage in an Age of Confusion*. New York: Norton.

Stern, D.N. (1998) *The Motherhood Constellation*. London: Karnac Books.

Stierlin, H. (1977) *Psychoanalysis and Family Therapy*. New York: Jason Aronson.

Stolorow, R.D. (1991) The intersubjective context of intrapsychic experience: a decade of psychoanalytic inquiry, *Psychoanalytic Inquiry*, 11: 171–84.

Stolorow, R.D. (1997) Dynamic, dyadic, intersubjective systems: an evolving paradigm for psychoanalysis, *Psychoanalytic Psychology*, 14: 337–46.

Stolorow, R. and Lachmann, F. (1984/1985) Transference: the future of an illusion, *Annual of Psychoanalysis*, 12(3): 19–37.

Stolorow, R.D., Brandchaft, B. and Atwood, G.E. (1987) *Psychoanalytic Treatment: An Intersubjective Approach*. Hillsdale, NJ: The Analytic Press.

Stolorow, R.D., Atwood, G.E. and Brandchaft, B. (eds) (1994) *The Intersubjective Perspective*. Northvale, NJ: Jason Aronson.

Strupp, H.H. (1988) What is therapeutic change?, *Journal of Cognitive Psychotherapy*, 2: 75–82.

Strupp, H.H. and Binder, J. (1984) *Psychotherapy in a New Key: Time Limited Dynamic Psychotherapy*. New York: Basic Books.

Thompson, M.G. (1994) *The Truth About Freud's Technique*. New York: New York University Press.

Timimi, S.B. (1996) Race and colour in internal and external reality, *British Journal of Psychotherapy*, 13: 183–92.

Turkle, S. (1995) *Life on the Screen: Identity in the Age of the Internet*. New York: Simon & Schuster.

Turner, R.M. (1993) Dynamic cognitive behavior therapy, in T. Giles (ed.) *Handbook of Effective Psychotherapy*. New York: Plenum Press.

Vaillant, L.M. (1997) *Changing Character: Short-Term Anxiety-Regulating Psychotherapy for Restructuring Defenses, Affects, and Attachment*. New York: Basic Books.

van Deurzen-Smith, E. (1988) *Existential Counselling in Practice*. London: Sage.

van Kessel, W. and Lietaer, G. (1998) Interpersonal processes, in L.S. Greenberg, J.C. Watson and G. Lietaer (eds) *Handbook of Experiential Psychotherapy*. New York: Guilford Press.

Warner, J. (1996) How does empathy cure? A theoretical consideration of empathy, processing and personal narrative, in R. Hutterer, G. Pawlowsky, P.F. Schmid and R. Stipsits (eds) *Client-Centered and Experiential Psychotherapy: A Paradigm in Motion*. Frankfurt-am-Main: Peter Lang.

Watson, J.C., Greenberg, L.S. and Lietaer, G. (1998) The experiential paradigm unfolding: relationship and experiencing in therapy, in L.S. Greenberg, J.C. Watson and G. Lietaer (eds) *Handbook of Experiential Psychotherapy*. New York: Guilford Press.

Watzlawick, P., Weakland, J. and Fisch, R. (1974) *Change: Principles of Problem Formation and Problem Resolution*. New York: Norton.

Weiss, J. (1993) *How Psychotherapy Works*. New York: Guilford Press.

Westen, D. (1988) Transference and information processing, *Clinical Psychology Review*, 8: 161–79.

Westen, D. (1991) Social cognition and object relations, *Psychological Bulletin*, 109: 429–55.

Wilkins, P. (1999) The relationship in person-centred counselling, in C. Feltham (ed.) *Understanding the Counselling Relationship*. London: Sage.

Williams, A. (1989) *The Passionate Technique: Strategic Psychodrama with Individuals, Families, and Groups*. London: Tavistock/Routledge.

Winnicott, D.W. (1965) *The Maturational Processes and the Facilitating Environment: Studies in the Theory of Emotional Development*. New York: International Universities Press.

Wolf, E.S. (1988) *Treating the Self: Elements of Clinical Self Psychology*. New York: Guilford Press.

Yalom, I.D. (1980) *Existential Psychotherapy*. New York: Basic Books.

Yalom, I.D. (1989) *Love's Executioner*. New York: Harper & Row.

Yontef, G. (1997) Relationship and sense of self in gestalt therapy training. *The Gestalt Journal*, 20: 17–48.

Yontef, G. (1998) Dialogic gestalt therapy, in L.S. Greenberg, J.C. Watson and G. Lietaer (eds) *Handbook of Experiential Psychotherapy*. New York: Guilford Press.

Young, J.E. (1988) Schema-focused cognitive therapy for personality disorders: part I, *International Cognitive Therapy Newsletter*, 4: 13–14.

Young, J.E. (1994) *Cognitive Therapy for Personality Disorders: A Schema-Focused Approach*. Sarasota, FL: Professional Resource Press.

Zetzel, E.R. (1958) Therapeutic alliance in the analysis of hysteria, in *The Capacity for Emotional Growth*. New York: International Universities Press.

# Index

Ackerman, N., 93
attachment, 54
    in couples and family therapy,
        96–7
    theory, 2, 47

Basch, F., 118, 122
Balint, 47
Beck, A.T., 62, 66, 67, 68, 69, 70,
    71, 72
Bion, W.R., 29
Bowen, M., 93, 95
Bowlby, J., 2, 47, 69, 96
Breur, see Freud, S.
brief psychodynamic psychotherapy,
    57–60, 61, 117, 123
    core conflictual relationship
        theme method, 58–60
    working with transference, 58–60
brief psychotherapy, 11–12
Bugental, J.F.T., 77, 78

cognitive behavioural therapy, 62–73
    affect, 66
    intervention, 67–8, 69–72
    projection, 72–3
    transference, 115, 118
    unconscious, 63, 64, 68
    working with transference, 64–5,
        69–72, 129

constructivist approach, 63, 68,
    109
containment, 29–30, 32
control mastery theory, 30
corrective emotional experience, 70,
    80
couples therapy, 92, 94–5, 103–12,
    118
    change, 107–12
    first order change, 109–10
    invisible marriage, 100–1, 107,
        108, 110
    second order change, 109–10
countertransference, 12, 69, 121
    in couples and family therapy,
        104–7, 118
    in existential therapy, 78, 80
    in intersubjective approaches, 56,
        57
    in object relations, 50
    in person centred therapy, 76
    projective identification, 31
cyberspace, see projection

Davanloo, H., 58
defences, 18, 30, 42, 73, 123, 124,
    126, 127
    definition, 20
    projection, see projection
dependency, 21, 71

drive theory, 46–7, 58
dysfunctional cognitive
    interpersonal cycle, 71

emotionally focused marital
    therapy, 17, 47
empathy, 7, 15, 75, 86, 116, 119
existential therapy, 74, 77–82, 86
    self disclosure, 82
    transference, 78, 79–82, 115, 118,
        129
experiential approach, *see*
    existential therapy

Fairbairn, W.R.D., 47, 49, 79
family systems theory, 93
family therapy, 92–4, 104, 108–9
    family of origin, 97–8
    history, 92–4
    internal working model
    projective identification
fantasy, 27, 28
Fenichel, O., 20
field theory, *see* gestalt therapy
fragmentation, 23–4
Frankl, V., 77
Freud, A., 41, 43
Freud, S., 2, 5, 8, 14, 19, 20, 30, 34,
    43, 45, 46, 58, 83, 115
    Anna, O., 36–7
    Breuer, J., 36–7
    childhood history, 35
    Dynamics of Transference, 37
    *Interpretation of Dreams*, 35
    libido, 38
    and transference, 2, 5, 35–41,
        115

Gelso, C.J., 4, 48, 56
gender, 21
gestalt therapy, 69, 72, 74, 82–5
    projection, 83, 85
    projective identification, 85
    psychodynamic theory, 84
    transference, 83–4
    unfinished business, 83

Gill, M., 3, 7, 11, 13, 15, 16, 76, 80,
    117
Goldfried, M.R., 64, 66, 67, 68
Greenberg, L.S., 79, 80, 90
Guntrip, H., 42, 47

Horowitz, M., 58
humanistic approaches, *see* person
    centred therapy

interpersonal expectancies, 66
interpretation, 5, 13, 14–16, 31,
    32, 37, 39–40, 49, 53, 78, 87,
    131–2, 133
    contemporary, 15–16
    in couples and family therapy,
        110–12
    genetic, 16
    here and now, 13, 15
intersubjective approaches, 55–7,
    60, 84, 115
    countertransference, 56
    working through transference,
        55–7

Kahn, M., 40, 41, 56, 76, 85, 90
Kernberg, O., 15, 33, 47
Klein, M., 26, 27, 34, 41–5, 47,
    133
    depressive position, 42–3, 44
    infants, 41–2, 43
    paranoid-schizoid position, 42,
        44
    phantasy, 42
Kohlenberg, R.J., 67
Kohut, H., 51, 52, 55, 76, 121, 122,
    133–4

Levensen, H., 58, 115
libido, *see* Freud, S.
Luborsky, L., 9, 58, 115

Mahler, 47
Malan, D.H., 58, 123
Mann, J., 58

Maslow, A., 77
May, R., 77, 78
Minuchin, S., 93
Moreno, J., 86

object relations, 8, 45–51, 53, 76,
    84, 86, 88, 89, 98
  definition, 47
  facilitating environment, 47
  good enough mother, 47, 96
  internal objects, 48, 49, 76
  object seeking, 47
  part object, 42, 47
  working model, 47
  working through transference, 49,
    50–1
oedipal, 8, 43, 58
Ogden, T.H., 27, 28, 31, 32, 33

person centred therapy, 7, 74,
    75–7, 130
  working through transference,
    76–7
personality disorder, 63, 65, 67, 68,
    69, 72, 79, 80
  borderline, 30, 49, 51, 65, 66,
    69–70, 79
  narcissistic, 30, 51, 65, 69
phantasy, *see* Klein, M.
phenomenology, 82
Pine, F., 47, 48, 49, 52, 54, 69
projection, 18–26, 30, 44, 85
  in couples, 20–1, 98–101
  cyberspace, 23–4
  definition, 18
  in daily life, 22–3
  families, 21–2
  functions, 19, 23
  infantile, 20
  psychological defences, 18, 20
  racism, 22, 23
  sexism, 22, 23
  splitting, 23, 30
  therapy, 22
  therapy groups, 24–6
  working through, 24–5

projective identification, 25, 26–33,
    44, 85
  in couples, 101–3
  definition, 26
  explanation of, 26–8
  importance, 30–1
  phases, 28–9
  supervision, 31
  unconscious process, 26, 29, 30
  working through, 29, 31–3
psychodrama, 86–90, 174
  object relations, 86, 88, 89
  sociometry, 89
  working with transference, 88–90
psychoanalysis, 8, 11, 32, 37, 40,
    41, 51, 52, 77, 78, 84, 93, 113,
    129
psychoanalytic theory, 7, 8, 41, 45,
    48, 51, 75, 76, 129
psychodynamic psychotherapy, 2,
    5, 41, 57, 58, 64, 68, 70, 71,
    94, 101, 107, 108, 113, 114,
    117, 129, 130

real relationship, 74–91
re-enactment, 30, 57, 79, 83
repetition compulsion, 2
  in brief psychodynamic
    psychotherapy, 59
  definition, 38–9
resistance, 13–14, 37
Rogers, C., 75, 76

Safran, J.D., 63, 68, 69, 70, 71, 72
scapegoat, 25
Scharff, D.E., 16, 48, 103, 104, 105
schema, 2, 6, 7, 63–6
  affect, 66
  cognitive interpersonal, 72
  conceptual schemata, 5
  core beliefs, 65, 71
  definition, 5, 64
  early maladaptive, 65
  irrational beliefs, 65
  mental representation of
    relationships, 2, 38, 39

organizing schemata, 4–5
script, 65–6
*see also* template
script theory, *see* schema
selfobject, 75, 121
self psychology, 7, 51–5, 60–1, 75,
 84
 empathic attunement, 53
 grandiose, 52, 53
 idealizing, 52, 53
 poles of the self, 52
 selfobject, 52, 121–2
 selfobject transference, 121,
  122–3
 transmitting internalization, 55
 twinship, 52, 53
 working with transference, 53–5
Sifneos, P.E., 58
splitting, *see* projection
Stern, D.N., 6, 21–2
Stolorow, R.D., 6, 55, 56, 115, 130
Strupp, H.H., 58, 72
supervision, 31, 113

template, 2, 5, 12, 38, 39, 47, 64,
 88, 115, 129
 couples and family, 95, 96, 106,
  107
 *see also* schema
therapeutic alliance, 7–8, 37, 56,
 95, 116, 117
 definition, 7
 in cognitive behavioural therapy,
  63, 64, 67–8, 69, 70, 71, 72
 in existential therapy, 79–80
 in gestalt therapy, 84
 in person centred therapy, 75
 in recognizing and responding
  to transference, 7, 32–3, 47,
  118–19, 121, 122, 124, 130–1
 ruptures, 2, 8, 30, 63, 71, 80
therapeutic frame, 116, 121
transference
 allusion to, 11, 12, 14
 as an organizing activity, 2, 5, 6,
  9, 12, 55, 84, 114

blank screen, 13, 40
change, 3, 13, 39
contextualized, 103–4, 106
definition, 2, 4–5
direct, 9–10, 12, 119
erotic, 37, 118, 119–21
explanation of, 1–4
focused, 103–4
Freudian psychoanalysts, 8
idealizing, 75, 122
indirect, 10–11, 12, 119
intersubjective schools, 9
mirroring, 52, 53, 75, 122
negative, 37, 117–19, 120
neutrality, 11, 12, 40, 76, 117
origins of, 6, 96, 115–16
persistent perceptions, 116–17
positive, 37, 117–19
recognizing transference, 117–28
relational schools, 8–9, 58, 130
significance, 6–8
triangle of conflict, 123–8
triangle of the person, 123–8
working through, 6, 11, 12,
  14, 49, 50–1, 53–7, 64–5, 66,
  69–72, 78–82, 85, 88–90, 129,
  131–4

unconditional positive regard, 70,
 118
unconscious, 5–6, 8, 11, 18, 19, 21,
 22, 26, 29, 30, 53, 58, 63, 64,
 68, 76, 78, 89, 96, 97, 98, 114,
 117
 in recognizing and responding to
  transference, 129–30

Weiss, J., 30
Winnicott, D.W., 47, 96
working alliance, *see* therapeutic
 alliance
working model, *see also* schema,
 template

Yalom, I., 77, 78
Young, J.E., 63, 65, 68, 70